THE ESSENES

AND CHRISTIANITY

THE ESSENES

AND CHRISTIANITY

An Interpretation of the Dead Sea Scrolls

DUNCAN HOWLETT

HARPER & BROTHERS   PUBLISHERS   NEW YORK

TO THE PEOPLE OF

THE FIRST CHURCH IN BOSTON

THE ESSENES AND CHRISTIANITY
Copyright © 1957, by Duncan Howlett
Printed in the United States of America

FIRST EDITION

C-G

Library of Congress catalog card number: 56-12067

CONTENTS

PREFACE

No one can hope to acknowledge all the indebtedness he incurs in writing a book of this kind. The works of the various scholars who have labored on the Dead Sea Scrolls and upon which I have chiefly relied appear in the Notes. There are, of course, others not directly quoted or cited, too numerous to mention.

Because I have tried to stay close to the Dead Sea Scrolls texts, there are a great many quotations from them included in this volume. Special thanks are due to the Viking Press for permission to quote from Millar Burrows' *The Dead Sea Scrolls*. I am also indebted to the Palestine Exploration Fund of London for permission to quote from the *Palestine Exploration Quarterly*, and to the American Schools of Oriental Research for permission to quote from the *Biblical Archaeologist*.

Over and above the best of books and journals, however, there are the living minds of people with whom we come in contact. Their influence is far more than we realize, and to them we owe the greatest debt of all. In this connection I should like to express my gratitude to Krister Stendahl and Immanuel Ben Dor, both of the Harvard Divinity School faculty, for the help and encouragement they have given me in my work.

How should a man acknowledge his indebtedness to his wife in the writing of a book? She made a searching analysis of an early draft; she read galley and page proof; she prepared the index, checked and numbered the footnotes, and so on. But such a list is the beginning, not the end, of his indebtedness to her in his work. Such is mine to Carolyn Chance Howlett.

DUNCAN HOWLETT

Boston
January, 1957

1

The Meaning of the Dead Sea Scrolls

Some two thousand years ago a little band of men known to history as the Essenes left Jerusalem, the capital city of their nation, and went out to dwell alone in the desert. They made their way down the Jericho Road, and on into the desolate region that lies at the north and west of the Dead Sea. There on the site of the City of the Sea of Salt, one of the six cities of the wilderness said to have been taken by Joshua and long since become a deserted ruin, they made their new home.

The Essenes left the comforts of urban Jerusalem and undertook the privations of desert life because of deep-seated religious convictions. They wanted to keep strictly to the traditional worship of Yahweh and to obey his Law. They objected to some of the practices and teachings of orthodox Judaism of their time on the ground that they departed from Israel's covenant with the Lord God. One might suppose that the religion of Israel, as taught by the scribes and Pharisees of the second and first centuries B.C., and as practiced at the Temple in Jerusalem by the official priesthood, left much to be desired. Quite the opposite was the situation. There probably never was a more devout or God-fearing people than the Jews of that period. It was, in fact, the very piety of Israel as a nation that produced the Essene movement. Groups of devout men and women have a way of evolving within their own number a minority that insists on yet more piety, a higher devotion to the ideal, stricter and more perfect worship of God. The Essenes were a passionately devout minority in a passionately devout nation, a natural product of a people who for generations had striven to do the will of God.

The thought and practice of these desert saints was described at length by Josephus, a contemporary Jewish historian, and by Philo, a contemporary Jewish philosopher. Pliny the Elder, a Roman, located them for us exactly. He wrote:

"Lying west of Asphaltites [the Dead Sea], and sufficiently distant to escape its noxious exhalations, are the Esseni, a people that live apart from the world, and marvellous beyond all others throughout the whole earth, for they have no women among them, to sexual desire they are strangers; of money they have none; the palm trees are their only companions."

The accounts of these writers and such others as have come down to us from the ancients are all static. None of them gives a hint as to the origin, the development or the demise of the Essenes. Modern archeology, however, has given us the story of their tragic end, which came in A.D. 68, some hundred and fifty years after they first went out into the desert to live. In that year Vespasian, the Roman Emperor, led the Tenth Legion into Palestine to put down a rebellion among the Jews. He destroyed Jericho, and at the same time apparently sent a detachment a few miles south to the Community Center of the Essenes built at the present-day Wadi Qumran and destroyed that too. A layer of ashes, found lying like a black quilt over the ruins, has told archeologists the story of the end. In all probability the members of the community were slaughtered or sold into slavery, if they were unable to flee. There is no trace of them afterward.

The Essenes appear to have foreseen the Roman conquest, however, and in preparation they carried to safety that which was most precious to them, their library of sacred writings. These were on scrolls, mostly of leather, as was the custom in those days. The Essenes had stored them in clay jars especially made for the purpose. So with the coming of the Romans they took their scrolls, jars and all, and hid them in caves which lay near their Community Center. These caves were located high in the limestone cliffs that rise above the plain in which the Dead Sea lies. They are almost inaccessible, and were originally quite invisible from the plain below.

The Essenes hoped to recover their precious library when the danger had passed. But no Essene apparently ever returned to claim these manuscripts. As all the world now knows, seven of their scrolls were found by chance by a Bedouin goatherd in the spring of 1947. Others have been found since that time. Thousands of fragments of yet other scrolls have also been found, and it is clear that even these are only a part of the whole.

Bits of information scattered through various ancient writings, widely separated by time, place and circumstance, suggest earlier discoveries of scrolls also from the Essene library. The first of these accounts occurs in the writings of Origen, one of the great scholars of the early church. In the third century A.D., he compiled a book of the various Greek versions of the Old Testament called the *Hexalpa*. In it he wrote of the discovery of biblical manuscripts in a jar near Jericho. Nobody can now prove that Origen was referring to a find in his time similar to the recent discovery of the Dead Sea Scrolls, but the parallel is too striking to permit of any other reasonable interpretation. Origen's statement is further corroborated by the fact that the Masoretes, the Jews who edited the authoritative Hebrew Old Testament, sometimes cited the "Jericho Pentateuch" as an authority. Eusebius and Jerome also mention it. Heretofore, no one knew what the Jericho Pentateuch was. Now it seems more than likely that it was an Essene work.

And that is not all. About A.D. 800, one Timotheus, the Nestorian Patriarch of Seleucia, wrote a letter to Sergius, the Metropolitan of Elam. In it he remarked that some trustworthy Jews who had been instructed in the Christian faith told him about some books that had been found in a cave near Jericho. After this discovery, according to the report, Jews from Jerusalem came in great numbers, and, searching the area, found books of the Old Testament and other manuscripts, plus two hundred psalms of David. Again the coincidence is too striking to be put down as mere chance. In fact, the similarity of the events of that time, 1,150 years ago, and today becomes almost too evident in the report that that discovery came by chance when an Arab hunter followed his dog into the cave where the manuscripts had been hidden.

Among the indications that there have been earlier discoveries of manuscripts from the Essene library at Qumran, none has given rise to more heated debate than the literature of a medieval Arab-speaking Jewish sect called the Karaites. The similarities between the Karaite literature and the Dead Sea Scrolls are acknowledged by everyone. But what do they mean? Relying upon these similarities, some scholars have been led to date the Scrolls in the Middle Ages in spite of the archeological and paleographic evidence to the contrary. Others have tried to determine the history of the Essenes through the Karaite writings.

It now seems clear that the Karaites were either influenced by or actually originated as a result of the discovery of Essene documents in A.D. 800. Their literature contains references to the Sadducees, the Pharisees, the Christians, and also the "Magharians." It is the mention of this last sect that gives us the strongest indication of a connection between the Essene library hidden in the caves of Qumran and the Karaites. "Magharians" is a translation from the Arabic and means "people of the cave." These people were so called, it is said, because their books were found in a cave.

The story of the Essenes as revealed in the Dead Sea Scrolls is ancient history. Yet it comes to us as fresh as a feature article in the latest issue of our favorite news magazine. The details that unfold before our eyes are all quite new. Through the writings in the Essene library, we begin to discover and we are now able to tell for the first time of the origin of these mysterious people in the remote history of Israel. We see the profound faith in Yahweh, the God of Israel, which completely possessed them and which animated all they said and did. Dimly, too, we see the outline of their great leader, the Teacher of Righteousness, and of his persecutor, the Wicked Priest at the Temple in Jerusalem.

We see the serenity and the holiness of the way of life they achieved. We see their beliefs developing and the rules being worked out by which they ordered their life together.

The Essene writings show beyond disputing how remarkable a group they were. Their fortitude, their singleness of purpose, their extraordinarily high moral standards, and their utter devotion to the God they loved and worshiped lift them far above the rank and file of men. Their independence of mind and their exultation of spirit distinguish them from their contemporaries in Israel and elsewhere. Few men have ever succeeded in following their convictions so completely, and even fewer have shown the determination to endure continuing privation for so long a time. Lastly, few men have been rewarded with a more intimate sense of common fellowship than the Essenes seem to have achieved in their life together in the desert.

The story of the Essenes is a thrilling and inspiring tale, but an account of their rise, development and tragic end, and their teachings and practices constitutes only half of the story. For when we examine what the Essenes wrote we discover that their beliefs and teachings show remarkable similarities to the beliefs and teachings of Jesus Christ. More startling is the fact that their writings reveal an even greater similarity to the thought and practice of the earliest Christian Church at Jerusalem.

The conjunction of time and place that is to be added to similarities in thought and language between the New Testament and the Essene literature has further heightened the excitement about the Scrolls. The Essenes were contemporaries of Jesus. While he was growing to manhood in Nazareth and while he was preaching in Galilee the good news of the coming of the Kingdom of God, the Essenes were living not far away in their Community Center by the northwest shore of the Dead Sea. Long before the discovery of the Dead Sea Scrolls it was suggested that Jesus might have spent the "hidden years" from the time of his presentation at the Temple at age twelve to the beginning of his ministry at about age twenty-seven among the Essenes. John the Baptist lived in the selfsame wilderness in which the Essene colony was located, and he baptized Jesus not far from the Community Center itself.

For Christian people everywhere, and for countless others besides, the figure of Jesus Christ has always seemed to loom up like a lonely island in the sea of history. Remote and inaccessible to the historian, he has throughout the centuries remained an object of faith rather than of knowledge in at least the ordinary sense of the word. We know him through the Gospels of Matthew, Mark, Luke and John, which are primarily works of faith rather than history, and through the Epistles of Paul and the Book of the Acts of the Apostles, which are also essentially works of faith.

In the discovery of the Dead Sea Scrolls, and the light they throw on Christian origins, it is as if we had quite suddenly come into possession of data regarding the geological formation beneath the ocean floor out of which rises the mysterious and beautiful island that so captivates our fancy. Now we understand, better than we had ever hoped, the underlying formations which endow the island with such majestic beauty. Now we can study the geological formations round about it, and perhaps discover the chain of events and the forces which thrust it up from beneath the waves.

Most important, we can perhaps now see that here, too, as John Donne said so long ago, "No man is an island." Now we can see, as never before, that the island we may have been tempted to think of as standing apart, unique and alone, rises out of subterranean formations of which it is an integral part. We learn that this island, with all its grandeur and immensity, is not a solitary thing at all, but that it is instead the apex of formations that heretofore we had been unable to see. We learn that these formations are continuous the world around. Thus we see that this island, of such peculiar significance to us, like every other island in every other ocean, is connected to all the rest by the great subterranean continents that stretch beneath the sea.

The Dead Sea Scrolls add nothing to our knowledge of Jesus, except that which may be gained through inference. In none of the manuscripts that has come to light is he mentioned. There is little likelihood of such a find, even if we assume a connection between him and the Essenes, because the Scroll literature was almost all written before his time. Nevertheless, the Dead Sea Scrolls have added an enormous amount of new data bearing upon the times in which Jesus lived, the influences that came to bear upon him, and the origin of the Christian Church. Herein lies their importance above all else. We had thought all the data that we should ever have in this area was already in hand, and that we could at best only restate and reinterpret it. Now, however, the entire field will have to be re-examined. Such a task is always difficult at best. It is much more so where matters of theology are concerned.

For this reason, more than one thoughtful person has ventured the prediction that the finding of the Essene library at the Wadi Qumran will prove to be one of the most important discoveries of the twentieth century. This statement is made with full knowledge of the amazing array of discoveries this century, now only half over, has already produced. They are the most promising documents having a bearing on Christian origins to come into our possession since the Renaissance. No manuscripts were more intently sought after during the Renaissance than those relating to the Christian Bible. Since that time the search for ancient biblical manuscripts has grown ever more intense—and ever less rewarding. By the end of the nineteenth century the great codices containing the whole Bible, Vaticanus, Alexandrinus, Sinaiticus and Bezae, had been analyzed and classified, as well as a host of lesser documents of varying age.

In the twentieth century there have been no significant biblical manuscript finds. Bible scholars have had to content themselves in analyzing and codifying what they already possessed. They have turned to digesting the earlier manuscript studies, and at the same time they have been attempting to integrate them with the wider discoveries of natural science.

Along with these efforts has been an attempt, continuing now for roughly a hundred years, to write the factual life story of Jesus, that is to say, to write the story as history rather than as theology. The effort ended in failure. As early as 1906, a brilliant young Alsatian scholar, the now world-famous Albert Schweitzer, published *The Quest of the Historical Jesus,* a volume in which he analyzed all the attempts to reconstruct the factual life story of the Nazarene. On completing his survey, Schweitzer declared flatly that it could not be done. There was not enough factual data to enable men to write a satisfactory biography of Jesus, he said. Thirty years later virtually every scholar had been brought to Schweitzer's conclusion. Since that time, only the novelists have continued the effort to write the life story of Jesus as one might write the life story of any man.

In recent decades, the theologians have consequently tended to emphasize faith rather than history. They have been concerned to show that the ancient faith remains inviolate, even when confronted by contemporary natural science and the cumulative critical studies of Bible origins. Important in this development has been the drying up of the sources of new data bearing upon early Christian history. New data of a historical nature calls for a readjustment in the fact scheme on which theology is based. The theological world, for example, was long in adjusting itself to the fact established by nineteenth-century scholarship, that the books of the Bible were written in different times and places by different men and for very special purposes.

The period in which there has been the greatest emphasis on the old theology has been the very period in which almost no new data has come in. The increasing emphasis on theological dogma has resulted in an ever-increasing unanimity of opinion among the theologians. We can see this trend in the frequent references of Protestant leaders to an "ecumenical theology," a theology in which the people of many different denominations, while holding to conflicting dogmas, can nonetheless agree.

Meanwhile the Christian Church—Protestant, Catholic, Eastern Orthodox—has never lost sight of the central figure of its religion. What history could not provide, faith through the doctrines and creeds of the churches supplied. For nineteen centuries the Church had wrestled with the historical problems about Jesus raised by the critical and the curious, the inquirer and the doubter. The cumulative answers to their questions that the churchmen have worked out make up the doctrines and dogmas of the Church. These have been tested in thousands of forensic contests; they have filled the spiritual needs of uncounted generations of men and have for centuries formed Western civilization's concept of man's ultimate nature and his place in the great scheme of things.

Then came the discovery of the Essene library, the now famous Dead Sea Scrolls. Their age and importance was recognized almost at once. Their relationship to Christian theology has been maximized, minimized, dismissed completely, and declared to be the end of Christian dogmatics. The true issues lie much deeper and are only now beginning to be seen. After many years of debate we realize that one of the great questions raised by the discovery of the Dead Sea Scrolls has to do with the fundamental relationship between dogma and fact; between faith and history. Which is to be given precedence? Which holds "truth"? Although this is one of the basic questions in all religion, it had ceased to be a live issue with us because all data bearing upon Christian dogma had been squared with it in one way or another. As a result of the finding of the Dead Sea Scrolls, however, the relationship between fact and faith has again been raised. Men are now asking the specific question, what is to be the place of the new data provided by the Dead Sea Scrolls in the official doctrines and creeds of the Church?

On one point we should be clear. The data that is coming into our possession as a result of the study of the Scrolls has been gathered with as much objectivity and scientific accuracy as contemporary methods of scholarship can attain. Most of the scholars at work on the Dead Sea Scrolls, an international team made up of Protestants, Catholics and Jews, may be said to be members of believing temples and churches. In certain quarters their "orthodoxy" has aroused the suspicion that the results of their work will inevitably be tinged with sectarian bias. It is alleged that their theological commitments are bound to color their studies. Such an assumption may seem valid on the surface, but it is wholly gratuitous, and is based on no evidence at all.

On the contrary, the passionate dispassionateness with which the very most orthodox scholars have sought to establish the data in regard to the Dead Sea Scrolls and not to prejudice their findings with dogmatic preconceptions is most reassuring to anyone who might suspect that dogma interferes with scholarship.

The theological viewpoint of the scholars frequently manifests itself in their writings, to be sure, but when it does, it does not intrude itself in the analysis of data. It usually appears in a sentence or a paragraph toward the end of the study and often sounds strangely irrelevant to everything else the author has said. The quarrel with the scholars, if any, is not that their theology colors their technical work, but that their theology seems to have made some of them very slow in moving to the conclusions toward which their studies seem to lead.

A number of writers, for example, have insisted that none of the information derived from the discovery of the Scrolls can affect religious faith. Statements like this often follow a long and careful analysis of factual material, the purpose of which has been to show affinities between the New Testament and the Dead Sea Scrolls, and the implications of which for dogma seem to be quite the opposite. Consequently readers receive the impression from such works that certain of the scholars, because of their theological predilections, are denying to themselves and to the public the most apparent implications of the data they have gathered. While they do not bend their conclusions in accordance with their theological dogmas, they nevertheless assert that their theology has not been and cannot be affected by their studies of the Scrolls.

Why is this so? Is it anxiety for the safety of some precious theological dogma that holds them back and causes them to say that no discovery can affect their theological position? So it has been argued. But the reticence of the scholars could quite as well be the result of scientific standards of the sternest quality—the unwillingness to aver that something is true when it is really only a shrewd guess. Such is the mark of true scholarship. We cannot have it both ways, although both may be true. Scholarly reticence in regard to the Scrolls may be due both to scientific standards and theological reticence. Any judgment in this area, however, is most unseemly. We may examine the evidence a man proffers, or we may examine his argument, and we may show where we believe him to be in error. But his motives for what he does are his own, and it is for us to leave them to him, as we would ask him to leave ours to us.

It is the purpose of this work to set before the reader some of the implications that may now reasonably be drawn from a study of the Dead Sea Scrolls, from archeology and from the writings of the ancients—our Bible, the Apocrypha, the pseudepigrapha, Josephus, Philo, Pliny and others. What is set down here is intended to be factual. It is based upon data that anyone may examine for himself and upon the conclusions the scholars have reached as indicated by their publications in learned journals. As far as possible the theology has been left out. It is the Scrolls themselves that tell the story. Readers are advised to turn to the translations which Millar Burrows has appended to his *The Dead Sea Scrolls* or to Theodor Gaster's *The Dead Sea Scriptures in English Translation.*

2

The Scrolls from the Qumran Caves

What are the Dead Sea Scrolls? Briefly the Dead Sea Scrolls are a vast collection of manuscripts found in 1947 and since in caves near the Wadi Qumran on the northwest shore of the Dead Sea. They consist of several complete or nearly complete rolls of leather, two rolls of copper, and thousands of leather fragments ranging in size from complete columns to scraps no larger than a fingernail. A manuscript roll, whether on leather, copper or parchment, is known as a "scroll." Hence the name "Dead Sea Scrolls."

Most of them were written probably in the first century B.C. Some can possibly be dated to the second, even to the third or early fourth century B.C. Some may belong in the first century A.D. At first there was a long and earnest debate among the scholars on the age of the manuscripts. It is now happily concluded. The evidence from paleography (the study of writing), from archeology (in particular from coins and pottery sherds) and even from modern science (the carbon 14 test) all points to the same general period.

More precise dating is now being attempted. Scholars are trying to discover which of the manuscripts belong to the earlier phase of the movement and which to the later. They are trying, for example, to determine when a particular manuscript is original, when it is a copy of an earlier work and when it is a writing that has undergone some editing. It is safe to say that as yet little has been accomplished in this field although these investigations when completed should prove to be very rewarding.

The Dead Sea Scrolls fall into three main divisions: (1) the complete or nearly complete leather scrolls, (2) the Copper Scroll, and (3) the fragments. We shall consider them in that order.

1. THE COMPLETE OR NEARLY COMPLETE LEATHER SCROLLS

Many people when referring to the Dead Sea Scrolls mean the rolls of leather found in the original cave in 1947, the story of which was told by Edmund Wilson in his *New Yorker* article and subsequent book. This is now known as "Cave 1." Considering their age, these scrolls are in a remarkable state of preservation and the writing on them may be clearly read. Their preservation is due to the very dry climate of the Dead Sea area and to the fact that the manuscripts had been wrapped in linen, like mummies, and stored in tall slender, pitch-sealed clay jars made expressly for this purpose.

The leather scrolls comprise only seven separate documents, two of the original seven having come apart where they had been sewn. These seven documents are:

a. The Book of Isaiah (complete).
b. The Book of Isaiah (incomplete).
c. The Commentary on Habakkuk.
d. The Manual of Discipline (two rolls).
e. The Genesis Scroll (originally called the "Lamech Scroll").
f. The War of the Sons of Light with the Sons of Darkness.
g. The Psalms (four rolls).

All are in Hebrew, except the Genesis Scroll which is in Aramaic. Hebrew, the literary language of the Jews at the time the Scrolls were written, was not used in everyday life. Aramaic was the living spoken language of the people. All of the leather scrolls are now in the museum of the Hebrew University at Jerusalem.

A primary value of the discovery of the Dead Sea Scrolls has to do with their bearing on our understanding of the Old Testament. Since this does not fall within the compass of the present volume, we shall go no further here than to point to the importance of all the Scrolls to Old Testament studies. The Old Testament manuscripts and fragments, which came into the possession of the scholars as a result of this fabulous discovery, are a thousand years older than any other extant Old Testament manuscripts in Hebrew. The great ancient codices of the Bible, containing both the Old and New Testaments and dating back to the fourth and fifth centuries A.D., are in Greek.

Thus the Dead Sea Scrolls have enabled scholars to reach behind our present Old Testament texts, the Masoretic (Hebrew) and the Septuagint (Greek), and to try to reconstruct the older traditions lying behind them. In the process they have been able to reassure us, on the evidence from the Dead Sea Scrolls, that our Old Testament texts, both Hebrew and Greek, have preserved the ancient traditions with astonishing accuracy and fidelity. Some corrections will, however, be necessary when a new translation of the Old Testament is made. Many small errors can now be corrected and many passages that were formerly quite meaningless can now be understood.

Of the leather scrolls, then, we shall consider only those that seem to have been original with the Essenes and which were unknown to us before 1947. They are:

The War of the Sons of Light with the Sons of Darkness

This scroll, the condition of which is almost perfect, is one of the smaller ones, being six inches wide. It is, however, more than nine feet long. It is made of three strips of leather carefully sewn together, and originally was wrapped in a covering of parchment. Other scrolls show indications of having formerly been covered in this manner, but their covers have long since become detached. The needle holes for the thread with which they had been attached may, however, still be seen on some of the manuscripts.

To suggest the flavor of the writing in the War Scroll, the

following, which comes early in the text, is typical. The systematic use of numbers is one of the qualities in the Scroll sect that has led some scholars to associate them with the Neo-Pythagoreans.

"During thirty-five years of service the battle shall be set in array six years, and those who set it in array shall be the whole congregation together. And as for the war of the divisions during the twenty-nine years that are left, in the *first* year they shall fight against Mesopotamia, and in the *second* against the sons of Lud; in the *third* they shall fight with the remnant of the sons of Syria, with Uz and Hul, Togar and Mashsha who are across the Euphrates; in the *fourth* and *fifth* they shall fight with the sons of Arpachshad; in the *sixth* and *seventh* they shall fight with all the sons of Assyria and Persia and the people of the east as far as the great desert; in the *eighth* year they shall fight against the sons of Elam; in the *ninth* they shall fight against the sons of Ishmael and Keturah; and in the *ten* years after these, the war shall be distributed against all the sons of Ham." (The italics are mine.)

Another typical passage reads:

"When they go to the battle they shall write on their standards 'The Truth of God,' 'The Righteousness of God,' 'The Glory of God,' 'The Justice of God,' and after these the whole order of the explanation of their names. When they draw near to the battle they shall write on their standards 'The Right Hand of God,' 'The Assembly of God,' 'The Panic of God,' 'The Slain of God,' and after these the whole explanation of their names. When they return from the battle they shall write on their standards 'The Extolling of God,' 'The Greatness of God,' 'The Praises of God,' 'The Glory of God,' with the whole explanation of their names."

So far the debate about the meaning of this particular scroll has been the least fruitful. Vain attempts have been made to find historical parallels to the war which the document purports to describe. The fact is that the schematic, magic number, ceremonial war which the scroll relates is unlike anything that ever could have taken place in heaven or on earth. We can recognize eschatalogical features and ascertain that it is an apocalypse of some sort. But it is not the kind of apocalypse with which we are familiar in writings of the same period, such as the Book of Enoch, the Book of Daniel, which is earlier, or the Book of Revelation, which is later.

It may well be that Krister Stendahl has found the key that unlocks the mystery in an Ugaritic writing of 1400 B.C., the so-called Keret text from Ras Shamra. There are many parallels between this ancient text, unearthed by French archeologists in 1929, and the War Scroll. The Essenes, of course, could not have known of the Ras Shamra writings which had long since vanished from the annals of human history. Only the science of archeology has enabled us to win them back from the limbo into which time gathers all things. The Ugaritic text is important because it shows a very ancient tradition for the bizarre kind of writing we find in the War Scroll. If the habit of writing in this highly artificial manner persisted among the Semitic people for more than a thousand years, we should expect to find it cropping out again exactly where we do—namely, in a group of ascetics who held the past in highest honor, and who apparently tended to regard a writing as sacred just because it was old.

General Yigael Yadin, noted archeologist and former commander-in-chief of the Israeli forces, dates the scroll by a study of its incidental military details. These details, he believes, do not represent the conscious intention of the writer whose mind was taken up with more important matters. Consequently, argues Yadin, they reveal such knowledge of military matters as the writer knew at first hand. A comparison of these details with the military practices of the ancients indicates to General Yadin, himself no amateur in such matters, that it was the Roman methods of the early Augustan period—the late first century B.C.—with which the author of the War Scroll was familiar.

To us, the Scroll may seem a highly schematized and wholly imaginary piece of writing. To the author, however, it was both practical and necessary. Its purpose, General Yadin believes, was to provide a manual of instruction to be used by the Children of Light at the end of days. Believing as he did that the end of days would be marked by a titanic struggle between the Children of

Light and the Children of Darkness, the author proposed to see that the Children of Light were prepared, and that they would know what to do when the time came. His ideas were derived from the Book of Daniel and the Book of Numbers in the Old Testament: from the Book of Jubilees and the Testament of the Twelve Patriarchs in the Pseudepigrapha and the current eschatalogical thought of his time.

In further support of his thesis, General Yadin recalls the Essene interest in books of warfare reported in Josephus' history as it is preserved to us in the Syriac language. He finds no inconsistency between their interest in war as shown by the War Scroll and their supposedly pacifist leanings. In calling them "pacifists" he believes we are reading our concepts back into their thought. They opposed human conflict and political warfare in practice but not in principle. They did so because they thought the end of days was at hand. In their minds there was only one war that counted and they chose to center their energies upon it. In their minds they were preparing for the conflict which should see the final triumph of righteousness and the eternal rule of God's elect.

General Yadin's theory makes sense. Nevertheless, while it has not been disproved, neither can it be said to have been established as the one true interpretation of the War Scroll. When we contemplate the steady progress in the world of scholarship, however, we do not doubt that where we are now ignorant, those who come after us will be informed. Obviously the author of the War Scroll had some particular purpose in mind. The writing has great meaning which we now cannot perceive.

The Habakkuk Commentary

When we turn to the Habakkuk Commentary, we are in the presence of quite a different kind of writing. It is one of the most informative and, consequently, one of the most rewarding of all the Dead Sea Scrolls. To be sure, it is not all transparently clear. Many of the references cannot be understood, while other references are subject to considerable dispute. Some, however, enjoy substantial agreement among the experts.

The Habakkuk Commentary is even smaller in size than the

War Scroll, being narrower and only five feet long. A portion is missing, a part scholars estimate to have been not more than six or seven inches. It is now about five and a half inches wide and is badly decayed along the edges. Apparently it was originally some seven inches wide. The text is one of the most beautifully written of all the Scrolls and the portion we possess is well preserved, indicating that it has been handled less than the great Isaiah Scroll, for instance, which shows considerable wear.

The following paragraphs comprise the first two sections of the Scroll and offer a sample of the writing. Unfortunately the beginning is lost. The commentary begins at chapter 1, verse 4, of our Old Testament Book of Habakkuk. The italics indicate lines quoted from the prophet by the commentator.

"So the law is slacked. This means that they rejected the law of God. *And justice never goes forth, for the wicked man encompasses the righteous man.* This means that the wicked man is the wicked priest, and the righteous man is the teacher of righteousness [1:4].

"Look among the nations, and see: Wonder and be astounded. For I am doing a work in your days that you would not believe if it were told. This means those who acted treacherously together with the man of the lie, for they did not heed the words of the teacher of righteousness from the mouth of God, and those who acted treacherously against the new covenant, for they did not believe the covenant of God but profaned his holy name [1:5]."

This kind of writing was by no means peculiar to the Essenes, the practice of interpreting Scripture going far back into the history of Israel. It was a natural result of the belief that their Bible was the word of God. Believing that God's will for them was to be found in Scripture, it was inevitable that the practice of emending and explaining obscure passages should develop. The Essenes, as we see in the Habakkuk Commentary, not merely continued the practice, but carried it further. In their interpretation of a passage they sought hidden prophecies of things to come.

The author of the Habakkuk Commentary was not attempting

to discover what the ancient prophet really had in mind, as is our practice. The Essene commentator approached the writings of the ancient prophet with a preconception of his own, and he read the ancient writing in the light of it. He believed that Habakkuk had the power to see into the future and that he gave voice in cryptic language to what he saw. If one had the skill, he could penetrate the surface of Habakkuk's prophecies and find there the story of events that were to take place long after the prophet's time.

This kind of writing, which, so far as we know, is peculiar to the Essenes, is called pesher by the scholars, from the Hebrew word "pesher" which is used to introduce each of the passages of commentary. It has been translated variously "Its meaning," "This means," "This refers to." As the Essenes themselves understood it, the word was used to indicate the fact that the commentator was stating the hidden meaning of a Scripture passage, known to the original author, but not heretofore revealed to anyone else. Thus the pesher of the Essenes, strictly speaking, is not midrash, it is not allegory, and it is not interpretation or commentary in the usual sense. It is the attempt to find in the Old Testament predictions of or references to a future time. In practice, the future of which they found the Scripture to be speaking was the time in which the Essenes themselves were living.

One who searches for hidden prophecies in ancient writings and succeeds in finding references to his own time is, unwittingly, reading the events of his own time back into the ancient writings he is interpreting. It was so with the Essenes. The commentator on Habakkuk, for example, knowing of the Teacher of Righteousness, attempted to discover a reference to him in Habakkuk's words. He also knew of the Wicked Priest, and he succeeded in finding a reference to him in Habakkuk also. Reading his commentary today, we see how fanciful his interpretation was and how much of his own personal knowledge he introduced.

For example in verse 8 he thought he saw a reference to the Romans or perhaps the Seleucids. Habakkuk, of course, had never heard of either, for he lived long before Seleucid and Roman times. The commentator calls the Romans the "Kittim."

"Swifter than leopards are his horses, and more fierce than ravening wolves. His horsemen advance proudly, they spread out; from afar they fly like a vulture swift to devour. They all come for violence; the aspect of their faces is an east wind. This means the Kittim, who trample the earth with their horses and with their animals; and from afar they come, from the coasts of the sea, to devour all the peoples like a vulture without being satisfied. And with wrath and indignation, with hot ire and furious anger they deal with all the peoples; for that is what it says: *the aspect of their faces is an east wind. They gather captives like sand.*" [1:8, 9]

The highly elastic nature of this foretelling of future events is evidenced in recent debates concerning the identity of the "Kittim." The effort to determine who the author meant by the "Kittim" has been very great, for if they could be certainly identified the dating of the events the commentator is describing would be made very much easier, and our knowledge of the Essene sect much more exact. In the effort to establish the identification, the Egyptians, the Macedonians (more specifically the Seleucids of Syria), and the Romans have all been put forward as likely candidates. Most scholars have held to one or the other of the two latter possibilities, with agreement more and more centering upon the Roman theory. The length and the intensity of the debate, however, shows that Habakkuk's words are vague enough to have enabled the commentator to find in them references to his own time, whether he lived under the rule of Antiochus Epiphanes, or a hundred years later under Rome. In fact he could have attached Habakkuk's words to almost any invading army that happened to suit his fancy, provided it was equipped with horses and could be said to have come from "the coasts of the sea."

The commentator showed his hand most clearly when, explaining 2:1-2, he wrote, "And God told Habakkuk to write the things that were to come upon the last generation." This is his way of explaining how it is possible for him to find in an ancient book prophecies of events through which his readers or perhaps their fathers had lived. Then he added, "But the consummation of the period he did not make known to him." That is, Habakkuk was given to know future events only up to the time when the commentator was writing. In this manner the author provided himself with a ready explanation of the prophet's limited foresight. Only the things that have already happened can be found in Habakkuk. Events that are to come after the time in which the commentary is written had not been predicted by the ancient seer. The commentator added that the Teacher of Righteousness has the ability to read the true meanings of ancient words, implying apparently that the understanding of the true meaning of the Book of Habakkuk must have come originally from the Teacher of Righteousness and not from the commentator. The commentator was evidently only the transcriber of the revelation.

While the Habakkuk Commentary is highly arbitrary in reading predictions of future events into the ancient prophetic writing, his observations are of the greatest value to us because they offer glimpses into the history of a sect that seems not to have recorded its own story elsewhere. Many of the events that the commentator found to have been predicted by Habakkuk and many of the persons he believed the prophet to have referred to would otherwise remain quite obscure to us, for only scattered references to them are to be found in the other writings that have so far come to light. The primary value of the Habakkuk Commentary for us is its history of the early phase of the Essene movement and particularly the Teacher of Righteousness.

The Manual of Discipline

While the Habakkuk Commentary is invaluable because of its historical references and because of the insight it gives into the beliefs of the Qumran sect, the Manual of Discipline provides us with a detailed picture of their practices and especially of their beliefs. If only one of the hundreds of scrolls in the Essene library could have been preserved to us, we should probably have chosen the Manual of Discipline.

The scroll as it comes to us has no name. The beginning is

missing. The manuscript is in two rolls, but they are clearly two sections of a single scroll. Originally it was six or perhaps seven feet long. It is one of the larger scrolls, measuring nine and a half inches in width. Five strips of leather have been sewn together. Like most of the others, it is in good condition and is clearly legible, although sometimes the top or bottom of a column is eaten away. It shows little evidence of usage.

The Manual of Discipline is a combination of directions, prescriptions, rules and notations for personal conduct, for carrying on the affairs of the community, for discipline, for admission to and expulsion from the order, and for worship. It is impossible to do it justice with a few quotations, but the following from the beginning of the Manual are selected to show the kind of writing it contains. There are some breaks in the writing, but no headings of any kind are included. They are inserted here in the interest of clarity.

The high purpose of the community:

". . . the order of the community: to seek God . . . ; to do what is good and upright before him as he commanded through Moses and through all his servants the prophets; to love all that he has chosen and hate all that he has rejected; to be far from all evil and cleave to all good works; to do truth and righteousness and justice in the land; to walk no longer in the stubbornness of a guilty heart and eyes of fornication, doing all evil; to bring all those who have offered themselves to do God's statutes into a covenant of steadfast love; to be united in the counsel of God and to walk before him perfectly with regard to all the things that have been revealed for the appointed times of their testimonies; to love all the sons of light, each according to his lot in the counsel of God, and to hate all the sons of darkness, each according to his guilt in vengeance of God."

How the candidate prepares himself for admission to the order:

"And all who have offered themselves for his truth shall bring all their knowledge and strength and wealth into the community of God, to purify their knowledge in the truth of God's statutes, and to distribute their strength according to the perfection of his ways and all their property according to his righteous counsel;

not to transgress in any one of all the words of God in their periods; not to advance their times or postpone any of their appointed festivals; not to turn aside from his true statutes, going to the right or to the left.

"And all who come into the order of the community shall pass over into the covenant before God, to do according to all that he has commanded, and not to turn away from following him because of any dread or terror or trial or fright in the dominion of Belial. And when they pass into the covenant, the priests and the Levites shall bless the God of salvation and all his works of truth; and all those who are passing into the covenant shall say after them, 'Amen, Amen!' "

The rite of initiation:

The priests shall recount the righteous acts of God in his mighty works and tell all the acts of steadfast love and mercy upon Israel; and the Levites shall recount the iniquities of the sons of Israel and all their guilty transgresions and sin in the dominion of Belial. Then all those who are passing into the covenant shall confess after them, saying 'We have committed iniquity, we have transgressed, we have sinned, we have done evil, we and our fathers before us, in walking contrary to the statutes of truth; but righteous is God, and true is his judgment on us and on our fathers, and the mercy of his steadfast love he has bestowed upon us from everlasting to everlasting.' "

Thereupon the priests bless all the members of the community, new and old, and the Levites utter a curse upon those who follow Belial. Curses of a particularly vituperative quality directed toward those who join the brotherhood and then leave it, are finally spoken by both priests and Levites.

The Manual of Discipline then turns to a consideration of the two spirits in man, the spirit of light and the spirit of darkness. We have already seen this point of view expressed in the War Scroll. Then follows a set of regulations by which life in the community is to be ordered. These are worked out in detail. It is not profitable for us to examine these, but the following lines give a true picture of the ideals that animate the rules, and the quality of life they were designed to engender and protect. It is declared to be the purpose of the members "to practice truth, unity and humility, righteousness and justice and loyal love, and to walk humbly in all their ways, that each may not walk in the rebelliousness of his heart or go astray after his heart and his eyes and the thought of his guilty impulse; to circumcise in unity the uncircumcision of impulse and the stiff neck, to lay a foundation of truth for Israel for the community of an eternal covenant, to atone for all who offer themselves for holiness in Aaron and for a house of truth in Israel, and those who joined with them for community and for controversy and for judgment, to condemn all who transgress the statute."

The Psalms

Among the scrolls found in Cave 1 at Qumran are four which contain only psalms. These make up a single large document, thirteen inches wide and having 39 lines to a column. There is no way of knowing how long the original scroll may have been. In all of its other dimensions, the Psalm Scroll is similar to the great Isaiah scroll. This would indicate that if it were of the same length, we have recovered only a fraction of the original. We possess some twenty distinguishable psalms, either in whole or in part. Gaster identifies nineteen, and many other fragments as well. They are not separated in the original, but they are identified by the opening phrase "I thank thee O Lord" or "Blessed art thou." Since all our quotations are from the translation of Millar Burrows, I have cited them according to the manner in which he has numbered them.

We have seen that the Manual of Discipline concludes with a psalm. It is in the same mood and style as those found in the Psalm Scroll. The following lines from it are typical of the Essene psalms taken as a whole:

> With the coming of day and night
> I will enter the covenant of God;
> and with the outgoing of evening and morning
> I will speak his decrees;
> and while they exist I will set my limit
> so that I may not turn back.

His judgment I will pronounce, according to my perversity—
for my transgression is before my eyes—
     like a statute engraved.
And to God I will say, "My righteousness";
to the Most high, "Foundation of my goodness,
Source of knowledge and fountain of holiness,
Height of glory and Strength of all,
to eternal majesty!"
I will choose as he teaches me,
And I will be pleased as he judges me.

When I begin to put forth my hands and my feet,
I will bless his name;
when I begin to go out or come in,
when I sit down or stand up,
and as I lie on my couch, I will sing aloud to him;
I will bless him with an offering of the utterance of my lips
more than the oblation spread out by men.
Before I raise my hand to satisfy myself
with the delights of what the world produces,
in the dominion of fear and terror,
the place of distress with desolation,
I will bless him, giving special thanks.
On his might I will meditate,
And on his steadfast love I will
lean all the day;
for I know that in his hand is
the judgment of every living man,
and all his works are truth.
When distress is let loose I will praise him
and when I am delivered I will sing praise also.

The Genesis Scroll

The condition of this scroll was such that it was unrolled only
with the greatest difficulty. At first it was called the "Lamech
Scroll" because the word "Lamech" could be read before unrolling. Some guessed that the scroll might be the lost book of Lamech
referred to in the Bible. When the unrolling was completed only
four full columns and five partial columns of script were recovered. There were some other single sentences and unrelated
words.

The scroll is a collection of apocryphal stories enlarging on biblical stories in Genesis. The part of the scroll that has been recovered is an Aramaic version of the narrative found in chapters 12-15. Most noteworthy perhaps is the fact that much of it is written in the first person singular, a practice that occurs only in late works like the Book of Daniel in our Old Testament and the Book of Jubilees in the pseudepigrapha.

As with the other Dead Sea Scrolls, the Genesis Scroll is reassuring to Bible scholars. The events related in these tales are the same as those found in our texts of Genesis, although greatly amplified. The events come in the same order, and proper names are the same, which shows that the author of the scroll was following a text that was virtually the same as the one we now possess. In fact, certain obscure passages and place names can now be better understood through the writing in this scroll.

An example of the type of material the scroll contains is a passage that expands Genesis 12:14-20. Our Old Testament relates that when Abraham went to Egypt with Sarah, his wife, he told the Egyptians that she was his sister lest, because of her beauty, they seize her and kill him. Sarah was made a part of Pharaoh's household, but because of it, great plagues afflicted the Egyptians. Discovering the cause, Pharaoh chided Abraham for his duplicity and returned Sarah to him with the words, "Now then here is your wife, take her and be gone." So reads the Bible story.

The Essene version of the tale expands the details considerably. "And how beautiful the look of her face . . . ," runs the description in the scroll. "And how fine is the hair of her head, how fair indeed are her eyes and how pleasing her nose and all the radiance of her face . . . how beautiful her breast and how lovely all her whiteness. Her arms goodly to look upon, and her hands how perfect . . . How fair her palms and how long and fine all the fingers of her hands. Her legs how beautiful and without blemish her thighs." One cannot help speculating on the presence of this rapturous writing, reminiscent of the Song of Songs, in the library of the ascetic Essenes at whose celibacy Pliny the Elder so greatly marveled. It may well be an argument in support of his observation, however, for none but a group of men who had laid all sensuality aside would be likely to include this kind of writing within a completely religious context.

In the passage Abraham then continues his story, relating it in the first person. According to this version, Abraham prayed to Yahweh to protect his wife and in answer "the Most High God sent a pestilential wind to afflict (Pharaoh) and all his household, a wind that was evil. And it smote him and all his house and he could not come near her nor did he know her." The account ends with Abraham's relating how Sarah was restored to him by the distraught king.

The Damascus Document

Even though it is not properly one of the Dead Sea Scrolls, the so-called "Damascus Document" must be included in our discussion. This manuscript which is written on leaves of parchment rather than rolls was found in 1895 in the genizah (manuscript repository) of a medieval synagogue near Cairo in Egypt. The document exists in two forms: manuscript A comprises eight leaves and manuscript B consists of a single leaf. The two manuscripts are not the same, but they overlap and supplement each other at certain points. The manuscripts are dated by the experts between the tenth and twelfth centuries A.D., although the date proposed for the actual composition of the Damascus Document as against the date when the copies we possess were made, range from the second century B.C. to the tenth century A.D. Before the Dead Sea Scrolls were discovered, most of the scholars agreed that the Damascus Document was probably composed in the first century B.C., or about the same time it is now known that the Dead Sea Scrolls themselves were written, a striking instance of the vindication of the methods of scholarship.

The Damascus Document is now classed with the Dead Sea Scrolls because of the close parallels between it and the Manual of Discipline and the Habakkuk Commentary. The similarity in thought and language permits little doubt that one is related to the other, or that all have their origin in a common source. What is clear beyond disputing is that whoever produced the Damascus Document produced the Dead Sea Scrolls, or that one of these documents was derived from the other, at least in part.

Furthermore, fragments from the Damascus Document have been found at Qumran, indicating at least that the Essenes were familiar with it.

2. THE COPPER SCROLL

In 1952, the so-called "Copper Scroll" was found in Cave 3 at Qumran. It lay on the cave floor in two separate rolls, and was so badly oxidized that at first no one attempted to unroll it. The feat was accomplished in 1956 by H. Wright Baker of the Manchester College of Technology in England, only by the use of the most extraordinary patience and technical skill. So completely oxidized was it that none of the original metal remained. After covering the scroll with airplane glue, he cut the oxidized metal into thin strips with a saw that was six thousandths of an inch thick. So carefully was the work done that none of the more than three thousand letters was lost.

There had been no little speculation as to why the Essenes should have chosen so unusual a material for writing. Copper was then both an expensive metal and also difficult upon which to write. The letters had, in fact, to be incised into rather than written upon the metal. The Copper Scroll is not, however, the only instance of writing on metal known from the ancient world. The Egyptians wrote texts on thin metal rolls and the Orphics wrote on gold plates. The plates were deposited in the graves of the dead as a kind of "passport" to the next life.

The reason why copper was chosen for this particular manuscript became apparent when the Copper Scroll was at last unrolled and read. Contrary to the expectations of almost everyone, the writing proved not to be biblical or sacred in any sense, but rather a record of buried treasure, in terms of our money amounting to some 200 million dollars!

Excerpts from the Scroll read as follows:

" (3) In the large cistern which is in the Court of the Peristyle, in a recess at the bottom of it, hidden in a hole opposite the upper opening: 900 talents (I, 6-8).

" (11) In the cistern which is below the rampart, on the east side, in a place hollowed out of the rock: 600 bars of silver (II, 10-12).

" (52) Close by, below the southern corner of the portico, at Zadok's tomb, underneath the pilaster in the exedra: a vessel of incense in pine wood, and a vessel of incense in cassia wood (XI, 1-4).

" (62) In the pit nearby, towards the north in a hole opening toward the north near the graves, there is a copy of this document with explanations, measurements, and all details (XII, 10-13)."

We are not concerned here with the question, does the treasure still exist and can it be found? The initial reaction of the scholars was sharply negative. According to the first newspaper reports they "were quick to say that the treasure probably does not exist" for they thought the amount "obviously fantastic," and they doubted that the treasure would have been buried at so great a depth of sixteen to eighteen feet, as the scroll says. Furthermore, the many legends of buried treasure in the East have so far proved false.

The Copper Scroll bears upon our problem only if it should prove to be a genuine record of treasure. That would add a very significant detail to our story of the Essenes. If the Copper Scroll is a true record and not imaginary, like the War Scroll, then we would know that the high priesthood of the Temple at Jerusalem once gave the fabulous treasure of the Temple into the keeping of the ascetic Essenes. The size of the treasure gives some measure of the importance of the trust. If this conjecture is correct, the treasure itself was probably hidden during one of the many sieges of Jerusalem, the record of it hurriedly beaten into copper because it was thought to be less perishable than parchment or leather, and then somehow given into the keeping of the Essenes.

If that date could be fixed, we should know much more than we do now about their relationship with the temple priesthood. It is, of course, possible that Cave 3 and its extraordinary contents were not known to the Essenes, but their extensive use of the caves in the immediate vicinity makes this seem very unlikely.

J. T. Milik of the French Centre Nationale de la Recherche Scientifique, to whom the decipherment of the Copper Scroll was assigned, is convinced that it has no connection with real buried treasure. "It goes almost without saying," he writes, "that the document is not an historical record of actual treasures buried in antiquity. The characteristics of the document itself, not to mention the fabulous quantity of precious metal recorded in it, place it firmly in the genre of folklore. The Copper Document is thus best understood as a summary of popular traditions circulating among the folk of Judaea, put down by a semi-literate scribe. He was, no doubt, one of the group of hermits who lived in caves nearby Khirbet Qumran, and presumably was associated with the Essene community. But it now seems highly unlikely that his work is in any sense Essene or 'official' as was generally presumed before the rolls were read. Rather it is a private effort, highly individual in character and execution, perhaps the work of a crank."

Milik does not discount the importance of the Copper Scroll, however. It can be dated by its script to the middle of the first century of the Christian Era, he says, and is for this reason significant for the study of Hebrew. "Here we have in the first century A.D.," he continues, "a text composed, not in 'biblical' Hebrew, but in a colloquial Hebrew dialect. The dialect in question has been known until recently only from later Jewish religious works, the oldest of which was the Mishnah. Just five years ago the first non-literary texts in 'Mishnaic' were found; these date from the Second Jewish Revolt (132-135 A.D.). The text of the Qumran Document is thus more than a half century older than the oldest texts in Mishnaic hitherto known."

3. THE FRAGMENTS

When the first of the Dead Sea Scrolls were discovered, and the Bedouin of the Judean desert were alerted to the possibility of further finds in that region, a feverish search of the area was begun. As a result, many other caves were found. Two hundred and thirty caves have now been excavated, according to Frank Cross, a leading authority on the Dead Sea Scrolls. When the archeologists caught up to the Bedouin and a systematic excavation was begun, thousands of manuscript fragments were found. More than ten thousand fragments were found in Cave 4. The laborious process of arranging, classifying and interpreting this mass of material is now in progress. How long it will take is a matter of speculation and what will be shown no one knows.

Originally the fragments were all parts of scrolls, like the large scrolls from Cave 1, and they were formerly part of the library of the Dead Sea sect that penned them. Consequently they, too, belong to the Dead Sea Scrolls literature. The importance they may eventually come to have is suggested in a monograph published by Cross in September, 1955. One of the larger fragments known as 4Q Sam b, a passage from I Samuel he discovered to be more ancient than any Hebrew script heretofore encountered. It may date to the fourth century B.C., he says, or possibly be as late as the second century. He places it conservatively between 225 and 200 B.C. The script is more archaic than that of the other Dead Sea Scrolls. Cross thinks it may have been a master scroll brought into the community at its founding. This fragment enables paleographers to reconstruct a far clearer picture of ancient Jewish handwriting than they previously possessed.

The fragment is important also because it agrees with the Septuagint (Greek) rather than the Masoretic (Hebrew) version of the Old Testament. Like so many other discoveries resulting from the finding of the Dead Sea Scrolls, it corroborates a surmise which the scholarly world made long ago, but had been unable to prove. Heretofore, it has not been possible to go behind the Masoretic text to the traditions out of which it was formed. But with this fragment, which is not much larger than a man's hand, we can go back four hundred years further, and, as a result, we learn that the Septuagint actually represents, at least in part, an older tradition than the Masoretic text. Thus the Book of Samuel is shown to be more authentic in the Septuagint than in the Masoretic text.

Much of the fragment literature was already known to the world of scholarship. This is reassuring because it means that we already have in our possession most of the works in the Essene library. Of those identified so far, ninety-two are biblical: thirteen of these are from Deuteronomy, thirteen from Isaiah and ten from the Psalms. There are also many fragments from the Apocrypha and others from the sacred writings of the Jews which were not included in the Old Testament or the Apocrypha. These documents as a class are called "pseudepigrapha" or false or spurious writings. They were so classified because they assume for themselves a sacred status that Judaism was not willing to grant them. Documents from the pseudepigrapha found among the Dead Sea fragments include eight from Enoch, three from Tobit and five from the Book of Jubilees. There are from the Essene literature proper, eleven fragments of the Manual of Discipline and seven of the Damascus Document; commentaries on Micah, Nahum, Psalm 37, with more identifications being made all the time. It is in the fragment literature that the new discoveries for the most part, are now coming in.

These, then, are the Dead Sea Scrolls, the manuscripts that have caused world-wide excitement. We shall now try to see what they reveal when studied closely in conjunction with the Old and New Testaments, the Apocrypha, the pseudepigrapha and the history of Israel.

3

THE ANCIENT HERITAGE OF THE ESSENES

The antecedents of the Essene sect can be traced back through a thousand years of Jewish history. Only in the light of that history can the movement really be understood. The ancestors of the Jews were a desert people. Sometime before 1200 B.C. they came pouring into Canaan and, having conquered the country, settled down and learned the way of life of the Canaanites. The details of the story are lost to us, but the central fact of the conquest and the settlement remains.

The invading Hebrews brought with them out of the desert a profound faith in their tribal god Yahweh. At first they doubtless believed in other lesser gods and spirits, as all ancient peoples did, but Yahweh, their particular deity, early became supreme for them. Far back in their tribal history they came to look upon him as their special protector and their leader in battle. At the same time they also began to look upon themselves as his people. He was their God alone and they, correspondingly, were his only people.

Coupled with their faith in their special deity was a faith in the immutability of the moral law. This law, as they conceived it, was simple, direct and elemental. It was the code of corporate life the desert nomads had developed by which to live together.

To them this law was no mere set of rules by which to get along with one another; the law was Yahweh's Law, given by him to his people through Moses, their great lawgiver.

The concept of a divine law was not original with the Hebrews. Many hundreds of years before, the Babylonians had engraved in stone a picture of their god handing their great law code to Hammurabi. Other ancient peoples in the Fertile Crescent held the same belief. The difference between the Hebrews and the others was in what they did with it. Among other nations the older idea that law came from deity gradually gave way to a belief that law is only a collection of precepts drawn up by men. Among the Hebrews, however, the belief that their law was God's Law not merely continued strong, but became a central tenet of their religious faith.

Many have thought that this single factor, a belief that their law was ultimately God's Law, explains the extraordinary vitality of the religion of the Hebrews as they emerge in the pages of human history. Credit for making the law central in Israel is frequently accorded to the religious genius of Moses, and none would discount his importance both as a lawgiver and as a leader who helped to center the faith of the people in Yahweh. Others have suggested that Israel's prophets, who, century after century, called the people back from their lax ways to the pure and undefiled worship of Yahweh, should be given the credit for making this belief central in Israel.

The one incontrovertible fact with which we begin is the intransigence of Hebrew religion in the face of the religion of Canaan. As the Children of Israel emerge out of the mists of myth and the haze of legend, we find them already imbued with a passionate devotion to their tribal god Yahweh. In other respects the Hebrew invaders took up the life of the people of Canaan whom they had conquered. They learned from them the arts of civilization and in time they became a society of farmers and artisans. As a result of the close interweaving of the two cultures, the Hebrews eventually absorbed some of the elements in the religion of the Canaanites. They began to worship Baal on the high places, as the Canaanites did.

The kings of Israel and Judah, whose task it was to maintain peace and order among the people, tended to be tolerant of the worship of the gods of Canaan, and tolerant of other lapses from the old tribal religion of Yahweh. If these rulers had been permitted to follow what undoubtedly seemed to them to be a wise and statesmanlike policy, the history of Israel would not have differed from that of half a hundred other nations that rose and perished in the two millenniums before the dawn of the Christian Era. But the kings were not permitted to do so. The special quality in Israel's religion that was hers alone produced a violent reaction to the permissive policies of the secular rulers.

The protest in favor of the ancient faith of Israel, the worship of Yahweh, was voiced by the prophets, a race of men who tower above the ages. The prophets of Israel were completely intolerant of any except the most rigorous adherence to the ancient way. The well-loved story of the contest on Mount Carmel between Elijah and the priests of Baal typifies the conflict that prevailed in that period, and the slaughter of the priests of Baal by the prophet of the Lord is probably as authentic an element as may be found in the Elijah story. The prophets claimed that the statutes of the Lord God permitted no compromise whatever.

Sometimes the prophets went so far as to foment rebellion if they found that a king was neglectful of Yahweh and could not otherwise be induced to mend his ways. It was Elisha who anointed a rebel king in Israel for the purpose of overthrowing the established monarchy. The prophets were not tender in their sentiments; they were fierce in their loyalty to the old religion. They gave no quarter and asked none. Elisha went beyond Elijah in his ferocity to root out the Canaanitic religion from Israel. He wrecked his vengeance on Jezebel and caused to be slain all who had supported the tolerant regime she and Ahab her king had fostered. Amos and Hosea rose in Israel and Isaiah and Micah in Judah continued to demand that the people hold to the ancient way. The kings were denounced for their apostasy, the priests of the Temple for their emphasis upon Temple worship, and the people for their sins.

Sometime in the course of the long contest between the

prophets of Israel and her kings, a wholly unique idea, that of the chosen people, became prominent. This idea was one of the strongest weapons in the arsenal of the prophets. At least as far back as Amos, they taught that the Jews were Yahweh's elect, living under a special covenant he had made with them. This covenant required the Lord to look upon Israel as his chosen people, and it required the Children of Israel to obey the Law which he had given to them by revelation through Moses.

That concept was either the cause or the result, or both, of the prophetic demand that Israel hold to her ancient faith. Both are cause and both are effect. The two ideas grew up together. Once formulated, however, the idea that Israel was God's chosen people became controlling. Through the prophets the entire history of Israel came to be viewed in the light of it. Such good fortune as Israel enjoyed was looked upon as the blessing of Yahweh, given as a reward for keeping the covenant. In the same way the sufferings and catastrophes which came to Israel were looked upon as punishment for the failure of the people to keep the covenant.

The prophets turned hindsight into foresight. Their philosophy of history became a threat. Israel had been accustomed to discover past sins in a present catastrophe, but the prophets taught the people to expect future catastrophe as a result of present sin. The prophets, measuring the actions of the people by the ancient Law, found them sinful, condemned them, and then added a dour warning. Unless the people changed their ways, Yahweh would punish them.

The prophets were vivid and concrete in their descriptions of future catastrophe, and all too frequently the worst of their predictions came true. Thus their philosophy of history established itself in the mind of Israel. When Samaria, the capital of the Northern Kingdom, was captured and destroyed by Shalmaneser of Assyria, it became clear to all pious Jews that the prophecies of Amos and Hosea had been terribly true. The destruction of Israel's capital was God's punishment of the Northern Kingdom for her sin. Consequently, when not long afterward Assyria again threatened, Hezekiah, king of Judah, became frightened. As a result of the warning of Isaiah that Judah, too, would fall if the people did not follow the Law of Yahweh, the king instituted a great many puritanical reforms designed to restore the pure and unadulterated worship of the Lord God of Israel. And to the astonishment of everyone, Jerusalem did not fall. Miraculously, so it seemed, the city was saved. Again the ability of the prophets to speak on behalf of the Lord seemed to have been demonstrated in a startling manner, and their authority was further increased.

Jeremiah, the most outspoken of all the prophets, demanded once again that Israel return to the ways of her fathers. Josiah, the king, thoroughly alarmed, made the observance of the Law yet more central in the religion of Israel. But Jeremiah could not be satisfied. He called for yet more righteousness, and continued to predict doom for Jerusalem. Even as he had foretold, doom came to the city. It fell to Nebuchadnezzar in 597 and again in 586 B.C. The words of the Lord's prophet were vindicated.

There was a further teaching of the prophets of which we need to take notice. It emerged among the later prophets who were confronted by an exiled people, the unhappy victims of all that the earlier prophets had predicted. God would save a remnant of the people, the prophets now said. On a great day yet to come Israel would be restored, the Temple at Jerusalem rebuilt, and Yahweh would once again be properly worshiped. While the people wept by the rivers of Babylon and asked how they could sing the Lord's song in a strange land, the prophets told them how and gave them new hope. God, they said, had not deserted his people. He had only tried them in the fire. Israel, his suffering servant, would be restored to its former glory. One of these prophets was Ezekiel, who had trained as a priest at Jerusalem before its fall. He laid heavy emphasis on liturgical practices and thereby helped to keep the little group of exiles loyal to the religion of their fathers.

In 538, Cyrus of Persia issued an edict by which the Jews were permitted to return to their homeland. The record is obscure, but apparently only a few of the most zealous took advantage of it.

They had no great means themselves, and they found the land desolate, and Jerusalem but a heap of debris. They erected a shrine on the site of Solomon's Temple, but attempted nothing more than that.

But again the voice of prophecy was heard, calling upon the people to keep to the ancient way. Haggai, a layman, addressed his words to the governor of Israel and the high priest. "Thus says the Lord," he cried, "the people say the time has not come to rebuild the house of the Lord. . . . Is it a time for you yourselves to dwell in your paneled houses while this house lies in ruins? . . . Consider how you have fared. Go up to the hills and bring wood and build the house, that I may appear in my glory, says the Lord." The work was begun at once as a result of his preaching.

Zechariah, a priest, took up the work of exhorting the people, and the newly rebuilt Temple was dedicated about 515 B.C. Still the work of the prophets continued. Still they continued to demand full allegiance to the religion of Yahweh. Worship was now centered in the Temple once more, but the priesthood grew corrupt, and Malachi arose to condemn them. When Nehemiah had rebuilt the walls of the city, Ezra, a Babylonian scribe, made a new demand that the religion of Israel be purified by dissolving all mixed marriages. The expected reaction arose against this kind of exclusiveness. It is expressed in the books of Jonah and Ruth, both of which are designed to show that Yahweh is a God of all peoples and that his concern reaches beyond the Jews.

So the ancient contest continued. Whenever Israel grew lax in her loyalty to the Lord God Yahweh, a prophet arose in her midst and in the name of the Lord called the people back to the beliefs and the practices of an earlier day. The prophets came from every walk of life, and they preached many and varied doctrines, but a single central theme is found in all of their messages. Israel is the Lord's chosen people and a covenant exists between the two. Yahweh will keep his part of the covenant if Israel keeps hers. The task of the prophets was to call upon Israel to keep the covenant, and, when she did not, to denounce priests, kings and people, and to warn them of the wrath that will follow upon their failure. It was out of this vigorous, puritanical, censorious, yet high-minded moral and spiritual stream of thought in Israel that the Essene movement and the Dead Sea Scrolls eventually came.

According to Jewish tradition, prophecy died out after 400 B.C. Apparently there was little in the religion of Israel after that time to which even a zealot might take exception. For more than two hundred years Israel lived at peace with herself and her neighbors under the rule of foreign overlords, Persia, Greece and Egypt. Her form of government was a theocracy, all her affairs, both civil and religious, being in the control of the Temple priesthood at Jerusalem. Her rulers were tolerant, and she was free to follow the precepts of her ancient faith as long as she remained subservient and paid the stipulated annual tribute.

When the empire of Alexander the Great broke up following his death in 323 B.C., the control of Palestine fell to Egypt. Again Israel became a sort of buffer state between two great rivals, as she had been in the days of the prophets. Now, however, the contending parties were Egypt in the south, ruled by the Ptolemies, and Syria in the north, ruled by the Seleucids. These two nations were political rivals, but culturally they were similar, for after Alexander, most of the civilized world sought to ape the culture of Hellas. Greek became the international language and Greek ways and modes of thought were everywhere adopted by cultivated people. It was a period of great commercial activity and of great mobility among people, particularly the well-to-do.

During this period, the third century B.C., many Jews went abroad to live and trade. A large colony grew up at Alexandria, the capital city of the Ptolemies. There amidst the cosmopolitan life of a great metropolis, they, like the rest of the people, accepted Greek ways and even gave up their native Hebrew language. Many of them were assimilated into the population of the city. Others, however, remained loyal to their own religion, although they adopted Greek ways, spoke and wrote Greek, and even translated their Bible into Greek. This translation, known as the Septuagint, eventually became the Old Testament of the Christians.

Thus Israel increasingly felt the impact upon her ancient

faith of the sophisticated Hellenistic culture of the ancient world. As a truly international civilization spread throughout the West, cultivated Jews more and more felt the limitations imposed upon them by their exacting religious culture. Outside Palestine they adapted themselves to it in various ways. In Palestine, and in particular at Jerusalem, however, there was no adaptation and no compromise between the two ways of life. The old conflict which had called forth the wrath of the prophets faced Israel once again. And again she had to choose between loyalty to her ancient faith and the demands of a new cosmopolitan culture.

The conflict reached a crisis in 175 B.C., when Antiochus Epiphanes came to the Syrian throne. Syria had by now wrested control of Palestine from Egypt. Antiochus was by conviction a determined Hellenizer and he believed that the forcing of Greek culture upon the various peoples of his empire would help to consolidate it. With the backing of certain elements in Jerusalem, he marched on the city and took it amid great carnage. He installed as high priest a "son of Aaron" with Hellenistic sympathies who thereupon undertook to enforce the policies of the Syrian monarch upon his own people.

Now the Hellenizing of Judea began in earnest. The high priest whose given name was Joshua took the Greek name Jason, began the introduction of Greek customs, built a gymnasium, introduced Greek games, Greek garb, and the Greek language. Many of the younger Jews eager to be rid of the ways of their fathers and to become like other people, were converted. Meanwhile, a deep and growing resentment was engendered among most of the Jews and particularly among those outside of Jerusalem who were unaffected by the broadening tendencies of urban life.

The true attitude of Antiochus Epiphanes became clear when he deposed Jason and put one Menelaus in his place. Menelaus had gone to the Syrian court and offered the king a higher price for the post of high priest than Jason had been willing to pay. Under Menelaus, the Hellenizing process was increased and resentment toward everything Syrian mounted to the point of controlled fury.

At this point war broke out between Egypt and Syria again. This, of course, meant civil war for Palestine once more. The pro-Egyptian Jews, fanatically loyal to the faith of their fathers, fought the pro-Syrian Jews who favored the Hellenizing of Jewish culture. The main body of the Jews were pro-Egyptian and fiercely hated their Syrian rulers. This antagonized Antiochus, who in the course of subduing his rebellious pro-Egyptian subjects, slaughtered unmercifully the people of Jerusalem and entered the Holy of Holies in the Temple, an outrage to the Jewish mind. As a final incredible offense to the Jews, he built an altar to Zeus on top of the Altar of Sacrifice in the Temple and then committed the supreme sacrilege of sacrificing a hog upon it.

The details in regard to the wars that followed need not concern us. The pattern is already familiar in the story of the times of the prophets. The old division persisted between those who favored cosmopolitan tendencies and those who demanded that Israel hold to the ways of her fathers. Again, as before, the internal religious struggle between the Jews themselves was complicated by the ambition of foreign powers to gain control of Palestine and to make her a vassal state. In the days of the ancient prophets, the contenders had been Egypt, Assyria and Babylonia. Now the struggle was between Egypt and Syria and subsequently Rome. Israel again was caught between the hostile armies. When at last the struggle was concluded, Israel had ceased to exist as a nation, the Essene sect had come and gone, and Christianity was already on the way toward the conquest of the Roman Empire.

With Antiochus Epiphanes as ruler of Syria and the master of Israel, with his Greek-minded puppet Menelaus holding the office of high priest, all Jewish practices were outlawed. It is impossible to conceive what that meant to pious Jews unless we keep in mind the long history of devout allegiance to the Law which lay behind them and the intensity of their conviction that Yahweh had made them his chosen people and that they must resolutely follow his precepts as recorded in their sacred books of the Law. Antiochus' men also went into the villages around Jerusalem where, accompanied by Jews of the Syrian party, they set up pagan altars. All Judea seethed in resentment and yearned to be free of so intolerable a yoke.

The Jews could bear no more. Under the leadership of an old priest named Mattathias, who had retired to the country, they again rose in rebellion. Before Syria had the chance to intervene, the rebellion took the form of a civil war of a truly fratricidal nature. The rebels turned upon and slaughtered every apostate Hellenized Jew whom they could lay their hands upon. No one who had co-operated with the Syrian rulers was safe from this reign of terror. When the Syrians attempted to put down the rebellion, the Jews achieved dramatic success against them. When Mattathias died, his eldest son Judas became the leader of the revolt. He struck with such force and fury that he became known as Judas Maccabaeus, that is, "the hammerer," the name by which he is known to history. The wars which he and his brothers carried on are called the Maccabean Wars.

Judas' first act was to cleanse the Temple at Jerusalem. He threw down the altar to Zeus and built a new one in it place. Sacrifice in accordance with ancient Jewish custom and practice was instituted once more. The rejoicing in Israel knew no bounds. The Lord had redeemed his people. The Temple and the high altar at Jerusalem had been restored to its former place in the religion of the people. Little Israel had repulsed the great Syrian Empire. A treaty of peace was signed, granting freedom of worship to Israel once more. Thus the rebels had won back the privilege of following the religion of their fathers without the interference of Syrian overlords. They had not actually wanted political independence, nor had they in fact achieved it. They were still subject to Syria as they had previously been subject to Egypt. But now they had the same religious freedom they had enjoyed under the Ptolemies.

Apparently, the most pious of the Jews wanted nothing more than this. It was a matter of no consequence who governed them so long as they were free to worship at the Temple and to follow the Law as they believed they should. There can be no other explanation for the fact that at this point, after religious liberty had been granted to the Jews, the most devout of them, known as the Hasidim, suddenly refused to support Judas, even though they had been his staunch allies in the war with the Syrians and quite possibly had been the instigators of the rebellion in the first instance.

As the lines of cleavage between the Hellenists and their opponents deepened, this group of men had emerged in Israel. The word Hasidim means "the pious." Our sources of information in regard to them are scanty, but it is clear that they were a religious, rather than a political, group. Theologically and probably socially conservative, they tried to live in accordance with the precepts of the ancient Law of their people. Their movement was a reaction to the increasing tendency toward Hellenism that resulted both from the pressures Syria brought to bear on the Jews and also the desire on the part of some of them to adopt the ways of the Greeks. Their course, apparently, was to hold strictly to the ancient piety themselves, rather than try to force the whole populace to do so. In this sense, there was an element of hopelessness in their program. Despairing of keeping all Israel loyal to the ways of their fathers, the Hasidim proposed only that they themselves should remain loyal to Yahweh's ancient covenant.

It is difficult to believe that the Hasidim would have refused continued support of Judas had they been able to see the dire consequences of their withdrawal from the political scene. Undoubtedly, like a great many religious purists, the Hasidim were theoretical rather than practical men. Tender of sentiment, they hated bloodshed, although they had indulged in it themselves when driven to desperation by the abominations of Antiochus Epiphanes. Now that their goal was achieved and the Law had been reinstated, they wanted no more earthly conflict and fratricidal strife. They left the Maccabees to the mercy of the Syrians abroad and to the Hellenists at home. Perhaps they were thinking of the theocracy under the Ptolemies. Perhaps they were harking back to the philosophy of Isaiah and Jeremiah who had counseled co-operation with, or neutrality toward, the foreign overlord.

Most probably the Hasidim withdrew their support from

Judas, once he had cleansed the Temple and re-established the ancient Mosaic Law in Israel, because they were millennialists. They were thinking of a kingdom not of this world. They were looking for the coming of the Day of Yahweh, the time of divine intervention when Israel would be redeemed of the Lord because the people had kept the covenant. Now was the time for them to put away the sword and by the strictest possible observance of the Law to prepare for the coming of the end of days.

In order to understand the mood and temper of those times in Israel, a reader should turn to the Book of Daniel. It is in that climate of opinion that the Maccabean Wars were fought and that the remarkable series of victories over the Syrian Empire were won. The Book of Daniel appeared in December, 165 B.C., and had undoubtedly been written just before that time. The book can be dated exactly because the history it contains, though vague at first, gains increasing clarity and accuracy of detail down through December, 165, after which time the details are simply wrong.

The Book of Daniel must have caused a sensation when it first appeared. In part it was narrative, relating the steadfastness of Daniel and his brothers in the face of persecution under Nebuchadnezzar and how the Lord intervened to protect them. The major part of the book, however, tells of a series of dreams of the future which Daniel had. In these passages are to be found veiled references to the time of the persecution of the Jews under Antiochus Epiphanes. Then it relates that at the "time of the end," when the Jewish people as a whole will be made to suffer in a similar manner, the Lord will again intervene on their behalf. The parallels to the Maccabean period, stated in allegorical fashion, are as clear to those who are familiar with the history of that period as they were to the Jews of the second century B.C.

There is probably no better explanation of the phenomenal success of the Jews in the Maccabean Wars than the Book of Daniel and the belief it generated among the Jews that the Lord God would intervene on their behalf if they kept the faith. It induced an apocalyptic mood among the people and made them fight with fanatical ferocity and bravery. Obviously the Hasidim accepted this philosophy, although they believed that fidelity to the Law rather than the use of the sword would bring about the promised salvation of Israel.

Their withdrawal of support came at a dramatic moment. Syria, as a result of her treaty of peace with Judas, was still the nominal ruler of Judea, although Judas was the ruler in fact. An issue arose over the high priesthood. The Syrian king had appointed one Alcimus to the post vacated by Menelaus, the hated high priest "who had the fury of a cruel tyrant and the rage of a wild beast," and who had been exiled and was later executed. Judas and the Maccabees, however, opposed the appointment because Alcimus was a Hellenist and because they were not willing to grant to Syria the right to appoint the high priest, a right they held to belong to Israel alone.

In order to see that Alcimus was duly installed in office, the Syrian monarch sent an army into Judea. Judas wanted to drive the army out of his country as he had so successfully driven out every Syrian army that had entered Palestine since the time he had taken command of the nation's affairs thirteen years before. Alcimus, like any political leader, attempted to undermine the position of Judas by assuring the Hasidim that he, Alcimus, would support their purist policies, even though he was by conviction a Hellenist. The Hasidim were satisfied. Dismissing as unwarranted and irrelevant the forebodings of Judas and the Maccabees, they recognized Alcimus as the legitimate high priest. All further resistance on the part of the Maccabees thus became useless, and Alcimus was installed by the Syrians.

Alcimus thereupon executed sixty of the Hasidim. The record is obscure. His motives are not clear to us. Obviously he intended to placate the Syrian monarch who had suffered so much at the hands of the revolting Jews. But what had these men done to provoke their execution by the high priest? Was the charge sedition? Alcimus doubtless made them appear as enemies of the state because of their determined opposition to all Hellenism. He presumably singled out the helpless Hasidim, who now could not and probably would not rebel, rather than the still dangerous Maccabees.

It is risky to make too much out of an event so lost in the

shadows of time. But we may assume that the execution of sixty of the Hasidim by a man who had promised to support them was a terrible blow to these religious purists. It was too late now for them to join forces with Judas and the Maccabees whom they had deserted. Sixty of their beloved had been killed by the man they had trusted. Where was the Lord God whom they had expected to intervene and save sixty of his most holy? This marked the end of their movement and we never hear of them afterward.

With the disappearance of the Hasidim the story of the Essenes begins. The Hasidim were not Essenes, and the Essenes were not the Hasidim. Each was a distinct movement. Yet, insofar as we can judge from the scanty evidence that has come down to us, the two were so close in their purpose and their general outlook that we are justified in saying that the Hasidim were progenitors of the Essenes. The Essenes took up the attempt to maintain the ancient piety of Israel that the Hasidim had begun. They carried Hasidist piety to the ultimate extreme of withdrawal from human society in order to preserve it.

4

THE ESSENE SECT IS BORN

Among the many ruins in Palestine that obviously date from ancient times is a mound near the northwest shore of the Dead Sea. It lies on a low bluff at the foot of the rugged limestone cliffs that rise from the sunken plain in the hollow of which is the Dead Sea. It is known to the Arabs as Khirbet Qumran or the "stone ruin," and stands at the Wadi Qumran. The mound was generally thought to be the ruins of an old Roman outpost dating from imperial times.

Nearby is a graveyard containing about a thousand graves, laid out in long parallel rows. A few graves had been excavated from time to time, but they yielded little information for they contained no artifacts. The bodies lie in shallow graves, face upward with the head toward the south and the feet toward the north, a practice that prevailed among the Karaites. Examination of the skeletal remains disinterred reveal the fact that several of them were of women.

Down to 1952, the sporadic investigations at Khirbet Qumran revealed nothing contrary to the view that it was an old Roman fortress. In that year, however, the discovery of the Scrolls in what we now call Cave 1 at the Wadi Qumran, coupled with the reference in Pliny to the Essene colony "lying west of Asphaltites," caused the archeologists to take another look at the "Khirbeh." In 1949, while excavators were at work at Cave 1, they explored the stone ruin a little, but again found nothing promising. When more and more caves, close to each other and ranged in a sort of cluster about the mound, were discovered near the Wadi Qumran, the archeologists decided upon a full-scale operation. Work was begun in the late fall of 1951 by the English archeologist G. Lankester Harding, and the French archeologist Père Roland de Vaux. The site was excavated a second time in 1952, and there have since been further excavations.

The results are little short of amazing. The foundations of a large building, obviously the community center of the sect that produced the Scrolls, were uncovered. The main building was 115 x 90 feet square, and constructed of roughly shaped stones, showing quite mediocre craftsmanship. A massive stone tower on the northwest corner of the building was erected, the archeologists supposed, for defense. The complex of rooms in the building included assembly halls, a scriptorium, kitchen, latrine, and other rooms the purposes of which can only be guessed.

A complicated water system included a large open reservoir. several smaller ones, many sumps or pools for drainage at the lowest part of a water system, and a patchwork of interconnecting channels between the pools. Some of the pools seem to have been used for ritual washing. The largest had broad steps by which people could have entered and left the pool, and there were others south of the building also equipped with wide stairways. These steps could have been used to get water, however. As the water level drops in cisterns used in the East, steps are necessary to make the water accessible.

It is agreed by the experts that the central building of the Essene sect dates to about 110 B.C., possibly earlier. This date means that we shall have to look for the events which brought about the building of the Essene Community Center at the Wadi Qumran and probably the actual founding of the Essene movement itself in the time of John Hyrcanus, 135 to 105 B.C. If we rely upon coins for the dates it can, of course, be argued that the building was not constructed until the reign of Alexander Jannaeus, 104 to 78 B.C., the theory being that a cache of coins from Hyrcanus' time had been carried to Qumran and used there in the later period.

We are now in a period about fifty years after Alcimus treacherously slew sixty of the Hasidim. The intervening years had seen bitter fratricidal strife among the Jews and almost constant warfare with Syria and occasionally with Egypt as well. Nevertheless, the Maccabean uprising succeeded, at least to a certain degree, and as a result, Israel became an independent self-governing state.

After the installation of Alcimus as high priest all the fears of Judas Maccabaeus in regard to him proved to be justified. We have seen the bitter disillusionment of the Hasidim whose withdrawal of support from Judas enabled Syria to elevate Alcimus to the office of high priest. Most of the rest of Israel felt equally bitter. While the Syrian kings kept the pact made with Israel at that time, which provided for freedom of worship, Syria never gave up her claim to rule Palestine, and never ceased her effort to reduce the Maccabees to the status of vassals of the Syrian crown.

Consequently, a contest for power between Judas Maccabaeus and Alcimus began almost at once. Soon Alcimus appealed to the Syrian king for help. Another army was sent into Palestine, but Judas met and defeated the Syrian forces in a pitched battle during which he lost his life. Alcimus, now in full control of the civil affairs of Israel, took the opportunity to avenge himself on his enemies, the followers of Judas.

Although he was a "son of Zadok," a descendant of one of Israel's priestly families, and although on accepting the office of high priest he had agreed to support the policies of the Hasidim, Alcimus now revealed himself as a true Hellenist. He relaxed the observance of the Torah, and went so far as to throw down the walls of the inner court of the Temple at Jerusalem. But he misjudged the temper of the average Jew. While there were Hellenists enough among them to constitute a strong and war-like party, the rank and file of the Children of Israel was out-raged. In their veins flowed the blood of generations of men passionately devoted to the following of the Law and they would tolerate no significant change in the old ways. When Alcimus died soon after, his death was generally regarded by the pious as the judgment of God upon him.

In the hills of Judea, meanwhile, Jonathan, another of the Maccabee brothers, had raised a new rebel force from the remnants of the army of Judas. Intermittent strife continued, the war with the Syrians went on, and the land knew no peace. Always Syrian interests were supported by the Hellenists, who were to be found largely among the priestly families of Jerusalem and who sought political power for themselves through Syrian intervention.

Jonathan, profiting by the experience of his brother Judas, would permit no one to be appointed high priest. The powers and perquisites of the office were so great that his own position as civil ruler would most certainly have been jeopardized. The office remained vacant for six years, but, because the religion of Israel required such an official, Jonathan was persuaded to accept the position himself. Simon, the last of the Maccabee brothers, followed Jonathan as both high priest and ruler of the state. John Hyrcanus, his son, succeeded him in both offices, although not without some difficulty.

John Hyrcanus was the first of the so-called Hasmoneans. Like his father, Simon Maccabaeus, and his uncles, Jonathan and Judas, John Hyrcanus was a devout Jew and intensely loyal to the ancient traditions of Israel. Following the practice established by his uncle Jonathan, he took the office of high priest, and like him, he also refrained from assuming the title of king.

Party alignments at this time continued very strong. On the one hand there were still the pro-Syrian Hellenistic Jews, and on the other, the devout conservative pious Jews, spiritual descendants of the Hasidim, who would permit no deviation from the old way. Both parties boasted many members who were "sons of Zadok," who, by virtue of their descent from Zadok, high priest under David, could claim the right to the high priesthood. In the middle were the Maccabees, the war party and the patriots, the rulers of the state, who strove to maintain the political independence of the little kingdom and to preserve inviolate the ancient religion of Israel.

By this time the men of the Hellenistic party had come to be known as the "Sadducees," a name derived from "Zadok." Why they chose the name we can only guess. There were quite as many sons of Zadok in the party opposing them. Since they were the liberalizing party, they probably took a name which suggested the authority and propriety that proper descent conferred upon them.

The opponents of the Hellenizing Sadducees were known as the Pharisees, a name which means the "Separators." It was obviously an epithet. Those who draw aside from the main body of men and strive to be holier than the common run, almost invariably elicit jeers for their efforts. Those who would not fight in support of the Maccabees and who would permit no modification in the archaic Jewish ways apparently came to be looked upon as "separators." The Pharisees were thus the party in John Hyrcanus' time that strove to hold Israel to the old prophetic ideal as had the Hasidim in the time of Judas Maccabaeus. Louis Finkelstein, the leading authority on the subject, says the Pharisees were the spiritual children of the Hasidim.

By the same token they were also the spiritual children of the prophets. There was, however, one conspicuous difference between the Pharisees and the ancient prophets. The Pharisees, even in the days when the movement was young, were a party which enjoyed considerable political influence in Israel. John Hyrcanus, devout Jew that he was, threw in his lot with them, and they, therefore, had the opportunity in accordance with their own lights of enforcing the Torah. The prophets had usually been lonely figures who in the name of Yahweh denounced the priest, king and people alike. Sometimes they enjoyed royal favor, but more often they did not. During this period, when prophecy was thought long since to have ceased in Israel the circumstances were curiously reversed, for under John Hyrcanus, the Pharisees who espoused the old prophetic ideal enjoyed the approval and the backing of the ruler of the state.

But John Hyrcanus was to abandon them eventually. Josephus

tells us that some time during the course of his rule John Hyrcanus gave a dinner for the Pharisees. When the feasting was
over he invited their suggestions and criticisms upon the god-
liness of his rule. All praised him except a single Pharisee,
Eleazar, who refused to join in the commendations and demanded
that Hyrcanus give up the office of high priest. "Since thou
desirest to know the truth," he said, "if thou wilt be righteous
in earnest, lay down the high priesthood and content thyself with
the civil government of the people." The record is by no means
clear, but Eleazar seems to have felt that it was wrong for a
ruler whose hands were stained with the blood of battle to offer
sacrifice at the high altar in the Temple. Josephus also indicates
that this lone objector voiced some doubts about Hyrcanus' true
descent from Aaron and Zadok.

The spirit of prophecy was apparently not yet dead in Israel,
for the demand of Eleazar was in the true prophetic tradition.
The reaction of Hyrcanus was according to tradition also. He
switched his loyalty from the Pharisees to the Sadducees, set
aside the Pharisaic religious ordinances, and forbade the observance of them. We can readily understand the position of each.
Eleazar would not compromise with what he regarded as the
religion of Yahweh. John Hyrcanus, on the other hand, found it
impossible to please such religious perfectionists as Eleazar. Nor
could he give up the office of high priest, thus jeopardizing his
rule in Israel. The Maccabees before him had learned that
lesson.

Another consideration probably played a part in the abandon-
ing of the Pharisees by Hyrcanus. While the Pharisees enjoyed
the support of the multitude, the Sadducees were still strong.
Tolerant and cosmopolitan in their outlook, they were a far
more congenial group than the zealous Pharisees and their demand for the enforcement of rigid ordinances. Hyrcanus would
naturally have considered switching his support to the Sadducees for a long time. Thus when his dinner for the Pharisees
was concluded, these religious zealots, who had enjoyed political
power and public favor, suddenly found themselves without
either. They who were the inheritors of the exacting tradition

of the Hasidim now saw their old enemies, the Hellenists, back in power.

This turn of events must have been humiliating to the Pharisees. More than that, it must have filled them with dismay. Devout believers in the Law, and accustomed to the use of political power to enforce it, they now found themselves in much the position of the Hasidim who fifty years earlier, after accepting Alcimus as high priest, were turned upon by him. Hyrcanus' sudden transfer of support to the Sadducees must have aroused memories in some of the older Pharisees, who may actually have witnessed the debacle under Alcimus.

When they had been abandoned by Hyrcanus, the Pharisees must have realized that the way chosen by the Hasidim, the way of withdrawal, was now the only alternative open to them. No longer could they hope to bring all Israel to a strict following of the Law through the exercise of civil authority. Both in thought and practice, the Hellenizing process had gone too far. Consequently, in the midst of the easy urbanity of Jerusalem, there was nothing for them to do but to continue to try to follow the Law themselves, leaving others to do as they chose. They alone, if necessary, would keep Israel's ancient covenant with Yahweh. At the same time they may have wondered if Temple worship itself was any longer valid, if there was doubt about the Aaronic descent of the high priest. It was probably during this period, when they tried to separate themselves from the ceremonial uncleanness of the rest of the people, that the inheritors of the old Hasidist philosophy began to be called Pharisees, or "Separators" by their countrymen.

The Pharisees, of course, did not completely succeed in their endeavor. They were surely forced to make some concessions in spite of their best intentions. It is difficult for religious groups to continue ancient religious prescriptions in the complicated society in which they live. As time passes, such rules become more archaic. The difficulty of living in a community that does not observe them increases. Only in a separate community, where all think alike and all desire to submit to the same regulations, can such practice be continued successfully.

We may be confident then that slowly and inevitably the Pharisees were forced to make a choice. At last there came a time when it was clear to them that they had either to compromise their ideal or to withdraw from society. Apparently there was a division on this issue, and out of this division among the Pharisees the Essene sect seems to have come into existence.

Those among the Pharisees who felt that it was possible to stay in Jerusalem and remain loyal to the Law became the real founders of the sect which still bears their name. Traditionally, the Pharisees were the party in Israel that sought to remain loyal to the ancient Law and yet by interpretation to show how it was possible to do so in an urban and changing society. The same exacting adherence to the ideal, interpreted in accordance with the practical problems of living, continued to characterize the best Pharisaic thought throughout the existence of the group.

Those who eventually withdrew to the desert and who are known to history as the Essenes were of the temper that tolerates no deviation from the old way. While the modifiers argued that their modifications were proper interpretations and emendations of the ancient faith, the literalists insisted that any such attempt was a compromise or an out-and-out departure, which could under no circumstances be permitted. It would be men of such temper who made up the group within the Pharisees that eventually became the Essenes.

Josephus records no such division among the Pharisees after John Hyrcanus' dinner. If we grant the likelihood of such a division after he switched his support to the Sadducees, we still need to explain why and how that split became so serious that the most extreme members of the Pharisaic party went to live in the desert by themselves. It seems unlikely that when the purists discovered that they could not bring all the Pharisees to their position, they would then have stomped off into the Judean wilderness. Such a decision would have come only after a long time, after they argued among themselves at length as to what course to pursue next. To explain their voluntarily undertaking the rigors of life in the desert, something more is required than the loss of political power and internal disagreement.

Again we find an answer in the history of Israel. While Josephus does not explicitly say that a new wave of Hellenization set in after John Hyrcanus threw his support to the Sadducees, he does record that the Pharisaic ordinances were repealed and that their observance was forbidden. This would mean the persecution of those who would not conform. Furthermore, old wounds heal slowly and the zeal of the Judaizers in rooting out the Hellenizers during the early Maccabean period must have left many a granulating wound among the members of the Hellenistic party that they were glad of the opportunity to avenge. We may certainly assume that enough reprisals followed to have been a source of suffering to many of the Pharisees. Persecution, together with the official repealing of the old regulations, would have made them yet more difficult to follow even by those predisposed to do so.

There was another factor. The expectation of the end of days, so clearly voiced in the Book of Daniel, increasingly dominated the thinking of the most religious of Israel's people at this time. Soon after the Book of Daniel made its appearance, the Book of Enoch appeared. Its purpose was to justify the ways of God to men and in particular to explain why God permitted so many things to happen which, by human standards of divine justice, should never have occurred. To achieve this purpose the author of Enoch, making liberal use of the Book of Daniel, confidently predicted the end of the world. At that time, he said, God will judge the world. The just shall live forever in peace and the wicked shall be destroyed.

This view was a reflection of a much more widely prevailing notion that history was cyclic rather than linear, and that the end of one of history's great cycles was at hand. A sense of impending doom was in the air. The Judgment Day seemed not to be far off. For those who believed in its coming, it was important above all else to be ready.

That this frame of mind was central with the Essenes we know from their own literature. This group of extreme purists went into the desert, among other reasons, to prepare for the coming of the Judgment Day, the Day of Yahweh, which they thought was imminent. If Israel, God's chosen people, would not prepare themselves for that awful time, these men at least, as a self-appointed latter-day remnant of Israel, determined to do so. Alone in the wilderness, they proposed to live according to the strictest possible interpretation of the ancient Law of their people.

They found in the writings of the prophet Isaiah the suggestion that they go into the Judean desert: "In the wilderness prepare the way of the Lord." They had tried to prepare for his coming in Jerusalem and they had failed. In the Scripture they found an answer. The Hebrew word, translated as "wilderness" in this passage, means not merely a dry and desolate region, but also the kind of depression in the earth in which the Dead Sea plain lies. We are not to conclude that they went into the Judean desert only because of this passage in Isaiah. It probably did not acquire full prophetic meaning for them until after they had actually begun their life there. But the clear import of the words could hardly have escaped them while they were making up their minds.

There were doubtless many deserted places to which these devout Pharisees might have gone besides the northwest shore of the Dead Sea, but we can discover a number of reasons for the particular choice they made. Proximity suggests one reason to us. It is scarcely twenty miles as the crow flies, from Jerusalem to Qumran. At the most it is two days' journey on foot. Most residents of Jerusalem must have known the region well. The Essenes would have been able to live in Jerusalem while supervising the building operations or even when helping in the construction.

Again the Wadi Qumran may well have determined their choice of a site in which to settle. A wadi is like a gutter, a river bed down which water pours in torrents when it rains and which is dry most of the rest of the time. The Wadi Qumran would have offered a source of water nearby.

Another reason for choosing that site was that the ruins of the ancient Israelitic City of the Sea of Salt were there. It had been abandoned hundreds of years before, but perhaps there were still some old building stones half buried in the ground which could be used. Perhaps the large number of caves in the cliffs nearby played a part in their decision. In fact, the community may well have begun its life in the caves and then, growing more prosperous, have built the stone house just above the plain.

Another factor ties into our story. John Hyrcanus was an able ruler. Israel enjoyed internal peace and prosperity under him. With such favorable conditions a religious movement would be able to develop and reach a point when at last it would be strong enough to establish itself in the desert. Conditions of war would make this development impossible.

It was a significant day for the world when the old uncompromising Pharisee Eleazar openly challenged the right of a political ruler of Israel to occupy the office of high priest. When the monarch refused to yield to his demands and withdrew all political support from the Pharisees, they were left with only such cause for continued existence as the power of their own religious convictions might call forth. From then on until the end of the reign of Alexander Jannaeus the Pharisaic party in Israel was forced to confine itself to religious and moral ambitions. After the manner of the prophets, some if not all of the Pharisees now stood apart from the organized Temple worship at Jerusalem and apart from the government of John Hyrcanus. In the name of the Lord God Yahweh, they henceforth dared to criticize both.

It is not suggested here that history hangs by a thread nor that without Eleazar and John Hyrcanus there would have been no Essenes, no Christ and no Christianity. The thousand years of the history of Israel, traced in the present chapters, are not to be denied. It was the peculiar character of Israel's long history that produced the crisis between John Hyrcanus and Eleazar. Had these two men never lived, the issue would surely have crystallized in some other way.

The Essene movement had its roots in one of the ancient and one of the high traditions of a great people. Its thought, mood and temper belonged to the greatest days Israel had known, the days of the prophets. The prophetic spirit was rekindled again in Eleazar. It burned again in the hearts of the strictest among the Pharisees, who by all human standards were already strict enough in their loyalty to the old way. They were like the prophets in the intransigence of their demand that Israel, as God's chosen people, remain loyal to their covenant with him. For this reason, when John Hyrcanus' dinner was over, currents were set to flowing out of which the Essene sect eventually emerged.

5

THE TEACHER OF RIGHTEOUSNESS

Few figures have made as sudden and dramatic an appearance on the pages of human history as the Teacher of Righteousness. Only a few scholars had ever heard of him before 1947. Their sources of information were so meager that he was generally thought to be a legendary or mythical character. He was mentioned only in the Damascus Document, discovered in 1895, and in the literature of the Karaites, the medieval Jewish heretical sect that probably owed its origin to an earlier discovery of documents from the Essene library.

In the opening portion of the Damascus Document we read that God "raised for them [the Essenes] a teacher of righteousness to lead them in the way of his heart, and to make known to the last generations, that which he would do to the last generation, the congregation of the faithless. They, the faithless, are those that backslide from the way." The Damascus Document also contains a reference to those who hold fast to the rules, who "go out and go in according to the Law, and . . . who give ear to the teacher of righteousness. . . ."

Other lines in the Damascus Document were generally supposed to refer to the Teacher of Righteousness, but there was no certainty and the scholars had little to go on. In fact, before the discovery of the Dead Sea Scrolls, the experts were not even agreed that there was any relationship at all between the Essenes and the Damascus Document. Although some came remarkably close to identifying the two, others were so wide of the mark as to have linked the "Covenanters of Damascus," as they were called, with the Sadducees, their bitter enemies. *The Encyclopedia of Religion and Ethics,* for instance, confidently stated two generations ago that "there is no difficulty in demonstrating the Sadducean affinities" of the Damascus Document.

The Habakkuk Commentary has left no doubt in anyone's mind as to the importance of the Teacher of Righteousness in the eyes of the Essenes. In it we read: *"The wicked man encompasses the righteous man* [Hab. 1:4]. This means that the wicked man is the wicked priest, and the righteous man is the teacher of righteousness." The commentary on verse 5 reads, "They did not heed the words of the teacher of righteousness from the mouth of God . . . for they did not believe the covenant of God but profaned his holy name."

Commenting on verse 12, the author condemns the men "who kept silence at the chastisement of the teacher of righteousness and did not help him against the man of the lie, who rejected the law in the midst of the whole congregation." And commenting on Habakkuk 2:2, he speaks of "the teacher of righteousness to whom God made known all the mysteries of the words of his servants the prophets." Commenting on verse 8 he says that God delivered the wicked Priest into the hands of men of his party. He finds in verse 15 of Habakkuk still another reference to "the wicked priest who persecuted the teacher of righteousness."

It is not always easy for us to be sure what the author means, for he implies much that his intended readers already knew and of which we are ignorant. This makes it difficult for us to catch his whole meaning, yet he tells us enough to reveal the elements in a great and tragic drama which he seemingly has known at first hand. The contending parties are two men, a priest of the Temple and a teacher of righteousness who had been a priest and who was thought to have the power from God to unfold hidden meanings in the words of the prophets. But it is quite clear that we are not witnessing a contest between two men only. Back of the Teacher of Righteousness are his followers and back of the Wicked Priest are his. In the mind of the commentator, in fact, the real contest is not between two individuals only or two groups. There is a dimension in which the contest is not merely human; it is cosmic. The eternal conflict of good with evil is embodied in this instance in the struggle between two of the sons of Israel. References to the Teacher of Righteousness in the fragment literature corroborate what we have been able to deduce from the Habakkuk Commentary.

What little we know with certainty of the Teacher of Righteousness may be stated in a few sentences. He was held in special reverence by the Essenes. He was a man of great piety and high moral character. At one time he was a priest. The Essenes regarded him as one who was specially gifted in unlocking the secrets of the Scriptures, particularly predictions of things yet to come. He suffered exile both for his beliefs and his teachings. Possibly he died as a martyr, although this is far from clear. Anything else that is said about the Teacher of Righteousness must be based upon conjectures derived from these and other relevant facts.

Did he found the Essene sect? Perhaps. Was he Eleazar, the Pharisee who challenged John Hyrcanus? Possibly. If so, did he then lead his followers out into the wilderness? Quite possibly he did, but not necessarily. We can be more certain that Eleazar or a younger disciple founded the sect and led the members into the desert than that either of them was the Teacher of Righteousness. Many a movement, founded by one man, has been given its form and purpose by a greater man who came later. The Maccabean revolt, precipitated by Mattathias, was subsequently led by his sons Judas, Jonathan and Simon. The Teacher of Righteousness could well have been a disciple of the founder, growing to greatness within the movement at Qumran and becoming a leader of the movement after the death of the founder.

The structure of the community, as we see it in the Manual of Discipline, provides for no such office as that of the Teacher of Righteousness. There was, to be sure, an overseer of the group, whose role was that of a manager or superintendent. Those of Aaronic descent enjoyed a certain pre-eminence. But this office was accorded little of the reverence which the Essenes gave to their Teacher of Righteousness. Perhaps if there had been such a Moses who led the Essenes out into the desert, he was not permitted to enter the promised land himself. Or, if he did, perhaps he did not live long afterward.

Another possibility is that the Teacher of Righteousness was neither the founder of the Essenes nor the leader of the group at any time. He was merely a member who was noted for his holiness, strict observance of the Law, and ability to find in ancient scripture prophecies of things that were happening in his time. He was perhaps not conspicuously more holy than the rest. What distinguished him was the fact that at Jerusalem, when the Law was flouted and wickedness prevailed, he dared to denounce the high priest to the people. If he did so, doubtlessly he suffered the fate that awaits men who are so bold as openly to defy established authority. Thus, becoming a martyr-hero of the sect, his deeds and his words thereafter became increasingly sacred to the Essenes. But we cannot certainly say that this was the case.

Except for the few scattered bits of information about the Teacher of Righteousness in the Habakkuk Commentary, the Damascus Document and the other documents we have mentioned, we have only two other sources of information about him. One is the literature of the pseudepigrapha, the holy books of the Jews, circulated at this time, but not a part of the Old Testament. We know that many of these works were read and treasured by the Essenes, for scraps from them have been identified in the fragment literature. Some scholars have thought they have found the Teacher of Righteousness described in the Testament of Levi and in other works as well. The phrase "Teacher of Righteousness" is, however, nowhere used in any of the pseudepigrapha that has so far come to light. In the absence of such direct evidence we are left with too little out of which to try to make a case by inference, that any of the characters described in this literature were in fact the Teacher of Righteousness of the Dead Sea Scrolls.

A second possible source of information about the Essene leader, so far almost entirely neglected, is the so-called "Thanksgiving Psalms." These are not the Psalms of David in our Old Testament, but the psalms which the Essenes themselves composed. The title "Teacher of Righteousness" is nowhere used in these writings, but when we bear in mind the reverence in which the Essenes held their leader, as shown by the Habakkuk Commentary and the Damascus Document, we are not just guessing if we search the Essene psalms in the hope of finding in them something that enlarges our picture of him.

The psalms are all in the first person singular. This by no means indicates that the Teacher of Righteousness is their author, but it suggests that he may have been. They may have been written by other members of the sect as if the Teacher of Righteousness himself had composed them. Only a writer who felt he knew something of the Teacher of Righteousness would dare undertake such a task. Thus we can assume that the Essene psalms may well contain dependable information about him. In ancient times it was not thought fitting for anyone except the king to speak to the deity in the first person. Only royalty could say "I" in speaking to God. Something of this mood may still have prevailed among the devout Essenes, addicted as they were to the most ancient standards and practices. In consequence they felt it quite proper to compose psalms in the first person, and then to attribute their work to the Teacher of Righteousness.

Most of the psalms may be found in readable translation in Millar Burrows' volume, *The Dead Sea Scrolls*. In the original manuscript, they are not divided and numbered as Burrows has done for the reader's convenience. Since his is the best known English translation, however, I shall, for identification purposes, refer to the psalms according to his method of numbering them. Psalm II reads as follows:

I was a trap for transgressors,
but healing for all who repented of transgression;
prudence for the simple,
and a sustained purpose for all those of a fearful heart.
Thou didst make me a reproach and derision to the treacherous,

a counsel of truth and understanding to those whose way is straight.
I became, against the iniquity of the wicked,
an evil report on the lips of oppressors;
scorners gnashed their teeth,
and I was a song to transgressors.
Against me the assembly of the wicked made a tumult;
they roared like the gales of the seas,
when its waves made a tumult
and toss up mire and dirt.
Thou didst make me a banner for the righteous elect,
an interpreter of knowledge in wondrous mysteries.
The men of deceit roared against me
like the sound of the roar of many waters.
Devices of Belial were their plans;
they turned to the pit the life of a man
whom thou didst establish by my mouth, and didst teach him;
understanding thou didst put in my heart
to open the fount of knowledge to all who understand.
But they exchanged them for the uncircumcised lips and alien tongue
of a people without understanding,
that they might come to ruin in their error.

Does not this psalm describe the kind of person the Habakkuk
Commentary shows the Teacher of Righteousness to have been?
The psalm seems not to have been intended to describe the trials
of an ordinary member of the sect as is the case with others of
them. Only the Teacher of Righteousness could have been
thought to look upon himself as "a trap for transgressors,"
"healing for all who repented," "a banner for the righteous
elect," and "an interpreter of knowledge in wondrous mysteries."
Such an utterance is in the tradition of Jesus and Paul, neither
of whom hesitated to make extraordinary claims for himself. At
least Paul did not, and those who came after Jesus did not
think it unseemly to put such words into Jesus' mouth.

If we compare Psalm II with what we know about the Teacher
of Righteousness from the rest of the Scroll literature, the resulting picture checks amazingly well and it amplifies our knowledge. We learn that he was a prophet in the ancient tradition of
Israel. Like Amos and Isaiah, he called upon the people to repent
of their sins. His preaching was accepted as wisdom by simple
people. His words strengthened those who desired to hold to the

ancient ways of Israel. He was a "sustained purpose" for those whose hearts failed when they were confronted by the wicked.

If we read the Psalms with the thought that they may describe the Teacher of Righteousness, even if they were not actually written by him, we find that, like the prophets, he incurred the ire of the civil and religious leaders of Israel. He openly denounced them as transgressors of the Law and they, on their part, sought to be rid of him. He called them "oppressors," "treacherous," "wicked," those of "uncircumcised lips and alien tongue" and "a people without understanding." They "gnashed their teeth" against him and accused him in "the assembly."

Then, like the prophets, the Teacher of Righteousness, if the Psalms describe him, felt the Lord God strengthening him. Psalm VII reads:

> While leaning upon thee
> I will rise and stand up against those who despise me,
> And my hand will be against all who scorn me;
> For they do not regard me,
> Though thou didst work mightily in me
> And didst appear to me in thy strength to enlighten them.

As an interpreter of knowledge in wondrous mysteries, the author of this psalm was a man who possessed the kind of special knowledge which the Habakkuk Commentary accords to the Teacher of Righteousness. It was apparently this which endowed him with the right to denounce priest and king, and it is this that sets him squarely in the prophetic tradition. He spoke not for himself, but for God. He was "a counsel of truth and understanding." Toward the close of Psalm II the psalmist is made to say of himself:

> Understanding thou didst put in my heart
> To open the fount of knowledge to all who understand.

According to the Essene Psalms, if they depict the experiences of the Teacher of Righteousness, his words, like the words of the prophets, "troubled Israel." Then, in retaliation, the leaders of Israel "circulated an evil report" against him and made him an object of "reproach" and "derision" among the people. "The men of deceit roared against me," the psalm says, "like the sound of the roar of many waters." Perhaps this means that they shouted him down when he tried to speak in the assembly. But nowhere does the psalm suggest that he was subject to anything more violent than verbal attacks. These, however, the Teacher of Righteousness seems to have felt keenly. The Psalms are filled with lamentations because of the attempt of the unrighteous to defame the singer and so to nullify the effect of his words. Apparently what the Teacher of Righteousness wanted most of all was to be heard and to have his words given respectful consideration in order that he might lead Israel out of her iniquity and into the way of righteousness.

Psalm XI reads:

> The lying lips shall be dumb;
> For all who attack me for judgment thou will condemn.

Psalm IV expresses a similar concern:

> They made me an object of contempt and reproach. . . .
> But thou, my God, didst succor the soul of the humble
>   and poor
> From the hand that was too strong for him . . .
> And didst not let me be frightened by their taunts
> Into forsaking thy service for fear of destruction by the
>   wicked.

If these words mean what they seem to mean, they give us a vivid human picture of the Teacher of Righteousness. Despised and rejected by his contemporaries, he yet contended with them courageously because the Lord God strengthened him. "By me," he adds, "thou hast enlightened the faces of many . . . for thou hast given me knowledge of thy wondrous mysteries." Here, surely, is the Teacher of Righteousness as the Essenes knew and loved him. This was the pattern, the belief and the ideal which became the lifeblood of the Essene community.

A careful reading of the Psalms gives us the exciting intimation that Eleazar himself may have been the Teacher of Righteousness. If he could have challenged John Hyrcanus to his face, why should we think that he later became silent? Josephus' story says that John Hyrcanus asked the Pharisees to set Eleazar's punishment. They suggested "stripes and bonds." This enraged Hyrcanus, for he thought Eleazar worthy of death. But Josephus does not say that Hyrcanus executed Eleazar, only that he thereupon abandoned the Pharisees and switched his support to their enemies, the Sadducees. That Eleazar was not executed at that time and that, in the tradition of the prophets, he continued and probably increased his denunciations seems more than likely, and it may be that we have corroboration for such a surmise in the Psalms.

In the Teacher of Righteousness we may have the final explanation of the exodus to Qumran. He, whoever he may have been, together with his disciples, finding life at the City of David no longer tolerable, went out from Jerusalem into the Judean desert. Objects of derision on the part of the populace, persecuted by the Sadducees, scorned and denounced by the main body of the Pharisees from whom they had separated, they must have considered flight to be the best course to take. Or they may have had no choice in the matter at all; perhaps they were simply driven out of the city. A line from one of the Psalms reads:

> I became a subject for strife for thy congregation, O Lord
> And contention to my friends.

Such had been the prophets of old. Such a one Eleazar would surely have been. Such a man the Teacher of Righteousness seems also to have been.

Beyond this point we cannot and need not go. The details in our picture may shift or vary or grow dim, but the broad outlines and the general line of development remain. We conclude that after the split between John Hyrcanus and the Pharisees and after the Pharisees subsequently split among themselves, the strictest of them, those whose piety would permit no modification in the following of the Law, made their way out into the desert and founded their own colony at Qumran. At some unknown time one of their members credited with special understanding, the power to interpret Scripture and to reveal mysteries, and possessing the will and the courage to denounce spiritual wickedness in high places came to be looked upon with great reverence and was called the Teacher of Righteousness.

6

THE WICKED PRIEST

The great antagonist of the Teacher of Righteousness was, as we have seen, the Wicked Priest. Our knowledge of him, like that of the Teacher of Righteousness, is very limited, for in the Scroll literature that has so far come to light he is mentioned only in the Habakkuk Commentary and in the Commentary on Psalm 37 in the fragment literature.

The problem in connection with the Wicked Priest is further complicated by the presence in the Scrolls of a number of apparently similar rascals who are variously designated. In the Habakkuk Commentary, for example, we find "The Preacher of the Lie" and "The Man of the Lie." In the Damascus Document we find "One who preached with lies," "The Man of Falsehood" and "The Man of Scoffing." In the Commentary on Nahum in the fragment literature there appears "The Lion of Wrath." In no case is the context clear enough to identify positively the persons referred to by these names as the Wicked Priest.

When all the references are considered, however, it appears that the Essenes had at least two quite different individuals in mind. On the one hand was the Wicked Priest and on the other was the Deceiver, a man who preached lies and falsehood and who scoffed at the Scroll sect. He seems to have led the people into backsliding and into "seeking after smooth things." The more we learn of this individual, the more it appears that he originally had the confidence of the Scroll sect but later became the leader of a group of malcontents. There is probably little chance of our identifying him with any known historical personage for the several references are too vague.

When we turn to the Wicked Priest, however, we are on more solid ground. We cannot be sure he was the Lion of Wrath. Some think he was, and others that he was not. We can, however, be confident that there was such a person who lived in Israel at one time and who persecuted the Teacher of Righteousness, although it must be acknowledged that here too a few scholars dissent. They argue that "Teacher of Righteousness" and "Wicked Priest" are to be looked upon as titles that apply to many individuals, in the manner that we use the word king or chairman. The view has little support, however, because among other reasons there are so many such terms. While we can easily think of these as epithets used to describe specific individuals, it seems quite preposterous to think of the Essenes not only designating one series of men as the Teacher of Righteousness, and another series as the Wicked Priest, but yet others as the Lion of Wrath, the Man of the Lie, and the Man of Scoffing.

Who was the Wicked Priest? If we can identify him we shall perhaps be well along the road to identifying the Teacher of Righteousness and to the dating of the origin of the Essene sect. In the unhappy period of Israel's history with which we are dealing, a time when brother was almost constantly at war with brother in a bloody fratricidal strife, the identification of the Wicked Priest is not as easy as we might suppose. There are several likely candidates for the dubious honor. Each attempted identification has been shown to be faulty. Opinion, however, seems slowly to be converging on Alexander Jannaeus as the most likely person. The Commentary on Nahum fragment, which speaks of the Lion of Wrath, makes this surmise seem more likely.

Certainly there is no one who fits the role better than Alexander Jannaeus. He was king and high priest in Israel from

104 to 78 B.C. His father was John Hyrcanus, who had come to rule Israel only because he had had the good fortune to escape a plot on the part of his sister's husband to murder him. In the plot Hyrcanus' father, Simon Maccabaeus, and both of his brothers were murdered.

When John Hyrcanus died, he bequeathed the government of Israel to his widow, and the high priesthood to his eldest son Aristobulus. This was in the year 105 B.C. Alexander Jannaeus, as the second son of Hyrcanus, got nothing. But he soon learned how dangerous it is to be in line for succession to a throne in turbulent times. Aristobulus, upon being installed as high priest, immediately imprisoned his own mother, his younger brother Alexander Jannaeus and all his other brothers. This is yet another illustration of the power which always came into the hands of the man who held the office of high priest. Aristobulus then made himself king as well as high priest. Within a year, however, he "died in agony," so Josephus says. Such was Alexander Jannaeus' introduction to the ways of men who desire power, and he learned his lesson at the hands of his own blood brother. How well he took these things to heart we shall presently see.

On the sudden death of Aristobulus, the control of Israel's affairs came into the hands of Aristobulus' widow, Alexandra, a most resourceful woman. She opened the prison doors, released the brothers of her dead husband and married the eldest of them who was Alexander Jannaeus. This made Alexander both the high priest and king of Israel. He inherited a small shaky domain that extended from the mountains of Lebanon in the north to the desert land south of Palestine and extended from somewhere east of the Mediterranean Sea coast to the region beyond the Jordan in the east. It is difficult to tell now just which of these east Jordan regions he actually ruled, but at best it was nothing more than an assembly of little principalities of subject people.

Alexander Jannaeus devoted the first nine years of his reign to campaigns in the east and south of his little empire, in an attempt to keep it in subjection and to extend its borders as far as possible. His methods were no better than those of any other warrior in those times. They could hardly have been worse. The barbarous cruelty of the victor in those days almost passes belief. But the effect of these campaigns, and the bloody manner with which they were conducted by the king of Israel, who was also high priest, outraged the sensibilities of the pious Jews. The Pharisees, in particular, who had found fault with John Hyrcanus, now looked upon Alexander Jannaeus as an utter desecration of their religion, their Temple, and the Law.

The extent to which feeling was mounting against him in Israel is made clear through an incident recorded by Josephus. In his role as high priest, Alexander Jannaeus was celebrating the Feast of Tabernacles on one occasion during this period, when he was pelted with lemons by the people. When we consider that he was standing at the high altar, the most sacred place in all Israel except the Holy of Holies; when we remember that in offering sacrifice to Yahweh he was engaged in one of Israel's most sacred acts; and when finally we remind ourselves that this happened at one of the most sacred times in the entire Jewish calendar, some notion of the pent-up feelings of the populace may be gathered. Very probably he had just previously been off at war for a long span of time, up to the elbows in the blood of those who opposed him, meanwhile neglecting his priestly duties at the Temple. No devout Jew could endure either of these patent offenses to his religion and his God.

Very possibly Jannaeus returned to Jerusalem at this particular festival for the special purpose of offering sacrifice in his role as High Priest. In any case, the pent-up fury of the people could no longer be restrained. Seeing him there, and led on by the Pharisees, the people showed their disgust and their shame in the harmless but thoroughly insulting fashion of throwing lemons at him. The act was not premeditated; it appears to have been quite spontaneous. The people had not come to the Temple having in advance armed themselves with rotten fruit. They had the lemons with them as part of their votive offerings, and flung them at him in anger rather than giving them up as offerings.

Jannaeus' response was characteristic of the man who is for

us the leading contender for the role of "Wicked Priest" in the Dead Sea Scrolls literature. Josephus says he slew six thousand men by way of revenge, and to impress the importance of his dignity and authority on the people. The figure may be exaggerated, but the savagery of Jannaeus' act cannot be. These were not warriors fomenting rebellion that he slaughtered with the aid of his mercenaries. They were his own people, his own blood kin. Furthermore, they were the most pious of his subjects, the most high-minded and the most moral. Those whom he slew were men who opposed bloodshed and who had expressed their outraged feelings not with the sword, but with lemons!

We have observed previously that we cannot say exactly when the strictest of the Pharisees divided themselves off from the main body of the group and went out into the desert to live apart from their capital city, separated from the Temple and completely withdrawn from the body politic. We have seen that they may have done so some time after the rift with John Hyrcanus, father of Alexander Jannaeus. But in the story of the lemons, we have still another instance of the fact that, however the details are worked out, the general outline remains the same. If the loss of political power under John Hyrcanus did not cause the Pharisee extremists to go out into the desert, certainly the slaughter of six thousand of the most devout among them would have done so. They might have fled to the desert for safety's sake if for nothing else.

If, however, the reader still is doubtful, if he wants to hold closely to the reported facts and does not think sufficient reason for the departure to Qumran has yet been found, there is more tragedy for devout Jews still to come which will surely provide all the motivation for going out into the desert the most exacting person could desire to find. Alexander Jannaeus had even more terrible things in store for those who dared to oppose him. Supposing himself to be more firmly established in his authority than ever before, the warrior priest now began a new war of conquest, this time against one of his Arab neighbors. In the course of it, however, he and his army were ambushed and he barely escaped with his life. In terror, he fled back to Jerusalem.

Now at last the time seemed ripe to be rid of him completely. The Pharisees who loathed him utterly as a man, and who yearned to avenge the death of the six thousand of their number he had slain in cold blood, now rose in arms against him. There followed six more years of bloody fratricidal strife of which Judea had already seen so much. Jannaeus relied upon his mercenaries and such Jewish support as he could get. The rebels fought fanatically and Josephus says that before this particular civil war was over fifty thousand Jews lay dead. One wonders whence came the manpower for the slaughter to which the Jews were so continuously subject during and after the Maccabean period.

What part did the Essenes play in this conflict? Our first answer to this question is that we do not know because we are not told in any of our sources. We cannot even be positive that they existed as a separate party at this time, 94-89 B.C., although the archeological evidence for the building of the Community Center at Qumran at an earlier date seems almost conclusive. We have in the Psalms ample evidence to support this view. They are filled with references that seem to have been written by someone who barely escaped the carnage of this period. The author of Psalm X cries:

> My eyes turned away from seeing evil;
> My ears from hearing blood
> My heart was appalled at the thought of evil
> For the worthlessness of a people is shown
> by the impulse of their being.

Josephus' estimate may be high when he says that fifty thousand Jews died in the course of Jannaeus' attempt to regain control of Israel, but again the measure of the man is not gained from the particular number of his own countrymen who died while opposing or defending him. His qualities and the light in which he was held by his contemporaries is to be measured by the wanton manner in which he decimated his own people in the effort to keep himself in power. We may add in his defense, for he needs what defense we can muster for him, that his methods were no more vicious than those of his contemporaries

who ruled the other kingdoms of the earth in the first century
B.C. Treachery and slaughter marked almost all of them.

Alexander Jannaeus was a true child of his time. It is his ill
fortune, however, not to be compared with his contemporaries
outside Israel, but with the Maccabees who preceded him—
Judas, Jonathan and Simon, and John Hyrcanus. Their wars may
have been as bloody, but their motivation was religious. Certainly this was true of the Maccabees. Hyrcanus marks the period
of transition. Strictly speaking, he was not one of the Maccabees,
but a Hasmonean. With Jannaeus and the rest of the Hasmoneans, the law of the Lord was virtually forgotten and conquest took its place.

At the end of six years of civil war, Alexander Jannaeus sued
for peace with the Pharisees. They, however, feeling secure in
their power, rejected the offer and demanded his death instead.
Then, in order to prepare for the inevitable reprisal by Jannaeus,
the Pharisees sent a delegation to their old enemy, the king of
Syria, asking him to intervene on their behalf.

In this extraordinary measure the Pharisees were doing again
what they and the Hasidim before them had done since the
early days of the Maccabees. Apparently they were again ready to
give over the control of the civil government of their land to a
foreign power in exchange for the payment of tribute and the
privilege of controlling their own internal affairs of both "church
and state" through the high priesthood. It would be interesting to
know how many of their countrymen supported the Pharisees in
the decision to ask the Syrian king to intervene. What we know
of the history of Israel at this time would suggest that nothing
like a majority of the people desired any such move to be made.

The king of Syria (now Demetrius III) of course, welcomed
an opportunity to have Palestine delivered into his hands. At
the head of a great army, he invaded Palestine, sought out
Jannaeus and dealt him a crushing defeat near Shechem. He
then prepared to move on Jerusalem and so to complete the
conquest of the realm. How few Jews had really supported the
Pharisees in inviting the intervention of Syria may now be seen.
Six thousand of them deserted the Syrian army and joined the
standard of Alexander Jannaeus!

No better illustration could be found of the tangled state of affairs that prevailed in Israel throughout the Maccabean and Hasmonean periods. The number of conflicting loyalties that beset every individual Jew as civil war after civil war raged up and down his unhappy land were almost impossible to resolve. We cannot be far from the truth if we say that one of the reasons why the Essene Community grew strong in this period was that it offered the devout Jew who loved the Lord the opportunity to serve him with singleness of purpose. Once at Qumran, he never had to choose sides again. There was only one side there, the worship of the Lord in the beauty of holiness. Back in Jerusalem, however, no matter what side he chose, the devout Jew found himself at one time fighting for something he abhorred, and at another, fighting against something he loved, and almost always fighting against his own blood brothers.

The feelings of the Essenes as they viewed these events seem to be mirrored in Psalm IX:

> I am comforted concerning the tumult of the people
> and concerning the uproar of kingdoms
> when they assemble against my counsel.

The Pharisees had overplayed their hand. The six thousand who deserted to Alexander Jannaeus when the Syrians prepared to march on Jerusalem, were obviously men who valued their national freedom more than the niceties of the Law and Temple worship. On the other hand, the Jews who remained with Demetrius' army were those who sought political power for the Pharisees under the rule of Syria, and who thought that in this way they could maintain the purity of Temple worship, and the strict following of the Law of the Lord. There is another curious element here. The part played by the Sadducees in this conflict is not told, but again, from what we know of them both before and after this incident, we can be confident that in the background they were fomenting the desertion to Jannaeus in a last desperate attempt to oust the Pharisees from the power which was sure to be theirs more or less permanently under the rule of Syria.

At this turn of events the Syrian king gave up his campaign.

He had trouble enough elsewhere to keep him occupied. If Palestine had now to be conquered with but a handful of Jews to support the campaign, it was not worth the effort. Demetrius consequently withdrew. That left Alexander Jannaeus once more in full control of Israel and the Pharisees completely at his mercy. But mercy was never a quality he had shown and certainly he showed none of it now.

In revenge, as well as to impress his subjects with the awful fate that awaited anyone who dared to oppose him, Alexander Jannaeus rounded up eight hundred men thought to have been the leaders of the revolt against him. These he crucified en masse, in a single night. Then, as if the agony of being left to hang upon a cross until death came at last were not enough, he caused the wives and children of these men to be slaughtered before their very eyes. Meanwhile, as a final affront, as one last ghastly twist of human savagery, he openly enjoyed himself with his concubines in the full sight of all. It was a night such as the world has seldom seen. Need we look further for the Wicked Priest of the Dead Sea Scrolls!

Corroboration for the role played by the Pharisees in this series of events is to be found in the fragment of the Commentary on Nahum. The references in this writing are more precise than almost any to be found in the Scroll literature. It contains many proper names, such as Jerusalem, Demetrius and Antiochus, and it refers to crucifixion "which was never done before in Israel." If "the Lion of Wrath" is Alexander Jannaeus, the Wicked Priest of the Habakkuk Commentary and the fragment Commentary on Psalm 37, the pieces of the puzzle fit so well that it is hard to believe they do not belong together. The Pharisees, who remained in Jerusalem, who fomented the rebellion against Alexander Jannaeus and enjoyed political control during the six years of civil war and who finally called Syria to aid them when Jannaeus threatened again, then would have been the "Seekers after Smooth Things." The Nahum Commentary refers to Demetrius, king of Greece, who sought to enter Jerusalem by the counsel of the "Seekers after Smooth Things."

Thus, in the Scroll literature, the Pharisees who would not

go to Qumran apparently are the backsliders and the scoffers, those who look at the fair neck and who are unwilling to give up all for the Law of the Lord. Their leader would then be the Man of the Lie, who sought to deceive the members of the Essene sect and tried to draw them into backsliding by giving up their ascetic life in the desert and returning to Jerusalem to enjoy political power there.

Josephus says that on that dreadful night in which Alexander Jannaeus wreaked vengeance upon his enemies, many Pharisees fled in terror from Jerusalem. Where would they have been more likely to go than to Qumran? Those who fled perhaps felt no little admiration for their sterner spiritual cousins who lived down by the Dead Sea. They wondered if the course pursued by the Qumran colony was not wiser, as well as better, than the one they had followed back in Jerusalem.

It would appear that the Essenes had two enemies: (1) Alexander Jannaeus, the Sadducees and the men of the war party and (2) the Pharisees with whom they were, however, really quite close. In a sense the Pharisees were the more dangerous because of their spiritual kinship and because of the constant practical political appeal that the Pharisees were able to make.

Nevertheless the Essenes at Qumran could hardly have failed to welcome refugees so close to themselves in thought, men who had witnessed such terrible things and had hardly escaped with their own lives. Whether the order was already so strictly organized that the newcomers were forced to endure the two-year probationary period required by the Manual of Discipline, we can only guess. Probably not, for the group would not long have been in existence as a separate unit at that time. We do not know whether the Community Center was full at this time. Possibly it was as a result of this new influx of members that the caves around Qumran first began to be occupied. And possibly it was in an attempt to intergrate the large number of new members that the stern rules of admission were devised. We can assume too that when Alexander Jannaeus' wrath was spent and life had become settled in Jerusalem, some of these new cave dwellers in the Judean desert looked longingly toward their former homes.

Some stayed, of course, but others returned to their old haunts and their old ways when it was safe to do so.

We can only guess the role that the Teacher of Righteousness played in these tragic and awesome scenes if indeed he played any. That he came into conflict with the Wicked Priest is clear. Undoubtedly, he denounced him first at Jerusalem and later at Qumran. Perhaps he did so openly in the city. He may have incited the lemon-throwing incident, which would be consistent with the character we know he possessed. Here we must leave the matter. The Teacher of Righteousness no doubt paid with his life. We cannot think that he suffered less for openly demanding that Israel's high priest-king live up in some measure to the requirements of his office. But how or when or under what particular circumstances, we do not know. We know why, and we also know the lasting effect of these events on the Qumran community. Indignation toward the Wicked Priest burns in the heart of the Habakkuk commentator even as his love, reverence and pity for the Teacher of Righteousness shines through the same passages.

Events such as we have been reviewing enable us to explain the curses and the hatred we find in the Dead Sea Scrolls. They do not seem to have a place in the hearts of the men who composed the documents we possess. They descend from the shattering experiences through which the founders of the sect passed. The same explanation may be given for the emphasis on the two natures in man, and for the strange preoccupation of one of their authors in a kind of schematic war between the children of light and the children of darkness. How else could those men have explained the presence of two such children of Israel as Alexander Jannaeus and the Teacher of Righteousness? In fact, how might they be explained better by anyone?

7

THE ESSENE COMMUNITY AT QUMRAN

What was life like at Qumran? Can we imagine how the Essenes established and carried on a community in the wasteland under the cliffs that rise from the bleak Judean plain just north and west of the Dead Sea? Can we visualize how they lived, how they managed their affairs, and how they wrung a living from the desolate region in which they had chosen to dwell?

Both Philo and Josephus have provided us with substantial information about Essene life and habits. The authenticity of these ancient authors was formerly questioned, but since the discovery of the Dead Sea Scrolls their writings have been given more serious attention. Such corroboration as the Scrolls have made possible indicates that they are remarkably dependable in their descriptions of the sect.

If, however, we are to continue our chronological account of the Essenes, the ancients will not be of much help to us as yet. Philo, the earliest of them, wrote either during the latter part of the first century B.C., or early in the first century A.D., at about the time of the birth of Christ. Pliny flourished about A.D. 70 and Josephus still later. Thus the picture of Essene life provided by these writers is some hundred to a hundred and fifty years later than the time of the founding of the colony at Qumran. Perhaps this is the explanation of the differences in the accounts of the ancients, as well as the differences between their accounts and the state of affairs the Scrolls seem to indicate.

An instance of such a difference is the statement of Philo that they live in "colonies," and of Josephus who wrote that "they have no certain city, but many of them dwell in every city." The records from Qumran suggest the existence of no other colony, unless the word "Damascus" in the Damascus Document implies the presence of a community there. Some think that the reference in the Damascus Document to "camps" indicates the existence of other Essene communities besides that at Qumran. Perhaps after the development at Qumran, Essene groups later grew up in many of the cities of Palestine.

If we rely primarily upon the Dead Sea Scrolls, however, we have less to go on, but there is still much that we can say. Nothing about them strikes us with so much force, perhaps, as the fact that the founders of the Qumran community were a singularly high-minded group of men. Only those whose religion was of paramount importance would have joined such an exodus. The hardihood and the devotion of this particular group of religious zealots can only be understood if we keep the rigors of life in the desert constantly before us. The extraordinary high-mindedness of the group is seen in the following passage in the Manual of Discipline:

"And these are their ways in the world: to shine in the heart of man, and to make straight before him all the ways of true righteousness, and to make his heart be in dread of the judgments of God, and to induce a spirit of humility, and slowness to anger, and great compassion, and eternal goodness, and understanding and insight, and mighty wisdom, which is supported by all the works of God and leans upon the abundance of his steadfast love, and a spirit of knowledge in every thought of action, and zeal for righteous judgments, and holy thought with sustained purpose, and abundance of steadfast love for all the sons of truth, and glorious purity, abhorring all unclean idols, and walking humbly with prudence in all things, and concealing the truth of the mysteries of knowledge."

Qumran was founded by a group of devout religious men, who were ready to endure the heat, the privation and the loneliness of life in the desert for the sake of the Law of the Lord as they understood it. This would make them as co-operative a gathering of men as one might hope to find, providing, of course, that their strict devotion to the Law was equal. If their major aim was kept in view, they would be well disposed toward one another and willing to subvert personal wishes to the common good.

Nevertheless, the group that founded the Qumran community were men and not angels. Undoubtedly they soon found themselves involved in the kinds of problems which rise in all groups of people, however high-minded they may be. The Manual of Discipline bears eloquent testimony to this fact. In order to function properly, any human society must have a set of rules to which all subscribe, or communal life is impossible. The Manual was obviously not composed at a single sitting. Earlier and simpler editions have been detected in the fragment literature. It was hammered out of the experience of a people who were learning how to live together and how to govern themselves. It contains the rules they evolved from their communal life.

We find then that the reference in the Damascus Document to the fact that the Essenes were at first "groping their way like blind men" to be a wholly congenial statement. It is unthinkable that they would at first have been the highly organized, tightly knit group that we see reflected in the Manual of Discipline. Only time could weld such a group into a strong organization.

The first rules would not have been written down. They would have been oral—the elemental principles of understanding which any group of men naturally accept. Gradually more elaborate traditions would be established. These in time would become the accepted practices to which each member agreed. Inevitably there would be lapses, for not everyone would live up to expectations. Thus it would be equally inevitable that some system of penalties or punishments would be evolved in order to hold all members to a common standard.

Then after older members had died and new members were admitted, the time would come when questions about the disciplines of the group would arise. More than one interpretation of the existing rules would be offered. When this happened the more important rules would be framed in written form. As more rules developed they, too, would be transcribed. Occasionally a complete revision of the rules might be made. Just such a document is the Manual of Discipline.

Thus life at Qumran created the Essene order in the form that we see it in the Dead Sea Scrolls. Had the extremist Pharisees not withdrawn into the desert, they never would have become more than another of the many parties and groups in Israel. Their withdrawal, however, created a community, the existence of which required rules and a governmental structure and endowed the individuals who were members of it with a group consciousness that they could not have achieved under less rigorous and confining circumstances.

A factor in the development of the group was the desire of others to join the colony. On what bases should new persons be admitted? Obviously not everybody could be allowed to join. Doubtless at first a tolerant policy made it possible for some who were not equal to the discipline of the group to be admitted. The disagreeable incidents that followed would then have required the group to question candidates with increasing care. At last the tight screening procedure seen in the Manual of Discipline was developed. The Manual, as has already been noted, called for a two-year probationary period for candidates.

The problem of defection arose to plague the Essenes. Proof texts from the Manual of Discipline support the statement. The Manual is explicit:

"Accursed for passing over with the idols of his heart may he be who comes into this covenant and sets the stumbling block of his iniquity before him, turning back with it, and when he hears the words of this covenant blesses himself in his heart, saying 'May I have peace, because I walk in the stubbornness of my heart!' But his spirit will be swept away, the thirsty together with the sated, without pardon. The wrath of God and the jealousy of his judgments will burn in him to eternal destruction; and all the curses of this covenant will cleave to him; and God will set him apart for evil; and he will be cut off from the midst of all the sons of light, when he turns away from following God with his idols and the stumbling-block of his iniquity. He will put his lot in the midst of those accursed forever."

"Falling away" is one of the greatest problems that sectarian groups face. Once a group has withdrawn from the common life of its place and time and has set up its own community whether in a separate place as at Qumran, or in the midst of society as with the early Christians, the pressures upon the members grow more intense, and the difficulties of maintaining the group increase. Society persecutes such groups because it distrusts them. This in turn increases the internal pressures within the sect. It tends to disintegrate. An outspoken desire on the part of some to return to the normal way of life makes itself felt, and the weaker members begin to fall away.

The measures which such a group takes by which to hold its members together, to enhance their loyalty and to fortify their courage in the face of persecution, are always strong. If they are not, the group falls to pieces. When, however, such measures are equal to the pressures they are designed to meet, the result is a further strengthening of the group itself. The sense of belonging increases and in consequence the sense of fellowship is increased also. A new bond draws them together. All have met the temptation of returning to the old way and have rejected it. They are now a group of individuals who have voluntarily accepted privation. After they have faced persecution, the sense of fellowship within the group is further increased. Relationships with the outer world are cut off when the members join; and their own relationships with one another are correspondingly strengthened.

All these things taken together tended to enhance the fellowship that prevailed at Qumran. There a group of like-minded men, who were not distracted by the quarrels of the outside world, lived together in close proximity, being animated by the same religious beliefs and endowed with similar spiritual qualities. Probably few men anywhere have gained a greater sense of fellow-feeling and have achieved a nobler quality of life than did the

Essenes. Philo attests to this when he writes:

"None of the treacherous and cunning tyrants was able to lay any charge against the company of the Essenes, or 'holy men.' Their moral excellence triumphed, and everybody treated them as independent and free by nature, praising their common meals and their indescribable good fellowship—the clearest proof of a life which is perfect and exceedingly happy."

It would be easy for us to idealize and to sentimentalize our picture of life at Qumran. We have learned a good deal from the archeological remains and from the Scrolls literature. We may conclude that life there was hard. The temper of those religious ascetics demanded such a life. They regarded poverty as a virtue in and of itself and the circumstances of the place and the time in which they lived would most certainly have imposed hardship upon them.

The question of water offers an illustration. Drinking water would be required all of the year. We know, futhermore, that ritual washing played an important part in the religious life of the sect. Most of the writing on the Scroll implies that these ritual washings took place regularly. Yet water was very hard to come by at Qumran. During the dry season, April through the summer, only the larger cisterns could have had water in them. In time these would have been exhausted. Some, in particular the smaller basins, would have grown stale and then foul. In the Manual of Discipline we have a clue that this actually happened, for the use of impure water for ritual washing is strictly forbidden. Only such water as they were able to store in the larger cisterns could have remained pure through the dry season. These hardy ascetics must have lived like a camel, which makes use of water when it is available and then gets along pretty much without it. One of the duties of the members may have been to fetch water from the spring at Ain Feshka a mile and a half from Qumran.

Nevertheless, life there was not impossible. If we find it difficult to believe that life could have been maintained in the Judean wilderness on so little rainfall—perhaps four or five inches a year—we have only to reflect that the entire kingdom of the

Nabataeans flourished at the same time in a most desolate neighboring region, by virtue of an elaborate system of ditches and catch basins. The ruins of this system may still be seen today in the region around Petra, Nabataea's capital city.

The food problem of the Essenes must have been similar. Nothing grows now, and nothing grew then in the summertime in the region around about Qumran. During this period the Essenes were confined to what food they had grown in the spring and dried for storage, or they would have had to fetch it from the green and fertile Jordan valley ten miles north or perhaps from the market place in Jerusalem or Jericho. Dried foods, perhaps embellished with such delicacies as locusts and wild honey, must have been their staple diet.

Even by the greatest ingenuity and the most unflagging industry, they could hardly have produced all the things they needed. They must have produced some kind of useful article which they could sell. That they were not without money is attested by the number of coins which the archeologists have recovered in the excavation of Khirbet Qumran. We know from the Manual of Discipline that individual members did not have money. Perhaps at the Center was a trading post where vendors exchanged products desired by the community for the manufactures of the Essenes.

What article did they make? The most obvious would seem to be pottery and manuscripts. Other industries of the homecraft variety may have been carried on at Qumran, but evidence of them has not as yet been found. We are, however, certainly within the realm of possibility when we surmise that the Qumran community supported itself by selling pottery and by copying manuscripts.

The evidence of a pottery industry may be observed at Khirbet Qumran. The scholars assume that the purpose of the manufacture of jars was for the storing of manuscripts. But the reverse is also quite possible. If the Essenes developed a skilled pottery-making industry, it may then have occurred to them that they might make jars to hold their precious manuscripts.

In any case their manuscript jars were most unusual. When

first shown two of them from Cave 1, Immanuel Ben Dor, who was in Jerusalem at the time the Qumran caves were discovered, said that the jars were most likely forgeries because they were unlike anything known to have come from Palestine in that period. The fairly complete pottery scale for Palestine in that period included nothing similar to the Qumran jars. Subsequent detailed study, however, readily revealed their authenticity to Dr. Ben Dor. He has since pointed to remarkable corroboration for the find in Jeremiah 32:14. "Thus says the Lord of hosts, the God of Israel 'Take these deeds [or books] both this sealed deed of purchase and this open deed and put them in an earthenware vessel, that they may last for a long time.' " Dr. Ben Dor points out that this verse probably refers to an ancient Hebrew practice that the Essenes revived. Almost identical jars, dating to the third and second centuries B.C., had previously been found in the Fayum region of Egypt containing rolls of papyrus. But the Essene jars are the only ones made for the purpose of storing manuscripts to have been found in Palestine.

A room or "pantry" containing quantities of clay dishes was unearthed in the ruins of Khirbet Qumran. The room may have been a storeroom where the pottery products awaited sale. We shall have more information when the pottery of Palestine is restudied in the light of what we now know about the pottery works at Qumran. To establish the group as craftsmen who sold the wares of a home industry, we shall need to find some of their handiwork among the thousands of sherds already in Palestine which date from the first century B.C.

There is less likelihood of our ever being able to establish definite conclusions as to whether or not the Essenes copied manuscripts for profit. That they had a scriptorium we know from the archeological remains that have been uncovered. The desks upon which they wrote and the ink wells in which they dipped their pens have been recovered. It can of course be said that the size of the Essene library is alone enough to account for the archeological remains relating to writing that have been uncovered. On the other hand manuscripts are perishable, which is, of course, a reason the Dead Sea Scrolls are so important. We do not possess other Palestinian manuscripts of the period. Yet may we not assume that the Essenes did what all men do when faced by the necessity of earning a living under new and difficult circumstances? They, no doubt, turned their hands to that in which they already had skill. Before the invention of the printing press, the tedious and difficult copying of manuscripts was a valued profession. The excellence of the writing in the Dead Sea Scrolls manuscripts testifies to the skill of the Essene scriveners. Even persons who do not read Hebrew, when examining a column from the great Isaiah Scroll, for instance, will see the consummate artistry with which the writing was done.

According to Josephus, the members of the Essene order wore white robes. Also, some of the Dead Sea Scrolls were found wrapped like a mummy, in linen cloth. Thus the Essenes may well have been manufacturers of linen cloth. Such an industry would have been very lucrative, for linen was always in demand and, when of good quality, brought a good price. On the other hand, they may have bought their cloth.

What matters is that we greatly err if we visualize the Essenes as sitting in idleness, merely contemplating either the blue sky or the ancient Law of their fathers. We know that they intently studied the Law. But our picture of them will be false if we do not also see them hard at work running their Community Center on a co-operative basis, farming in the spring when there was rain enough to raise crops, and making products which they could either exchange or sell for the things they themselves needed. Josephus says they thought it a good thing to be "sweaty."

One of the most remarkable qualities of the Essene community was the degree of equality achieved among the members, a quality hardly known in the ancient world, except among groups like the Stoics. A. Dupont-Sommer, a French scholar, has observed, "How eloquently the ideas of liberty, equality, and fraternity are proclaimed in this religious society." In support of this statement, he cites the passage in the Manual of Discipline which provided that each member of the community should have the right to vote on all questions, and he adds a quotation from

Philo relating to their condemnation of slavery. All of the members participated in the assembly, the so-called "Sessions of the Many," when the voting was done. Let us refer on this matter to the words of the Essenes themselves, as translated by A. Dupont-Sommer:

"Now this is the procedure for a Session of the Many. Everyone according to his rank! The priests shall sit down first, and the elders second, then the rest of all the people. Let them sit each according to his rank, and equally let them interrogate with regard to judgment and for all manner of counsel and of any matter which concerns the Many, each bringing his knowledge to the Council of the Community. No man shall interrupt the words of his fellow before the other has finished speaking. Neither shall he speak before his proper order, [before] he who is enrolled before you, [before] the man who is being examined. Each shall speak in his turn. And in the Session of the Many no one shall speak any word which is not according to the pleasure of the Many, and at the request of the man who is the overseer of the Many. And every man who has something to say to the Many, if he is not in office, the man who wishes to examine the Council of the Community, this man shall rise to his feet and say: 'I have something to say to the Many.' If they bid him he shall speak."

To the foregoing paragraph from the Manual of Discipline, Dupont-Sommer adds a quotation to amplify the text from Josephus who said of the Essenes: "Nor is there ever any clamor or disturbance to pollute their house, but they give everyone leave to speak in their turn."

The equality which the group achieved came as a by-product of the circumstances by which the group was formed rather than as a policy instituted in accordance with an abstract principle. The principle undoubtedly came out of practice rather than vice-versa. The group of Pharisees who withdrew from their fellow Pharisees and went out into the desert were as we have seen probably a group of equals or near equals. Not all were sons of Zadok. But all were of like mind. Either they did not want servants to go with them, when they withdrew into the desert, even though many or most of them had been accustomed to having servants, or their servants would not go with them; or if they did, they later became equal members in the order.

Probably most of the members were not priests, however. Some of them seem to have been Levites, the Temple servants, although this is not clear either. Obviously they were generally well-to-do even though not enjoying very great wealth, otherwise they would not have had the resources with which to build themselves so pretentious a stone building. It is not of the best workmanship, to be sure, but that can easily be accounted for by the fact that once having decided to build their center they were eager to occupy it, and also that it would have been difficult to persuade good workmen to go out into the Judean desert to labor. No doubt they did much of the work themselves in the manner of pioneers.

Thus a homogeneous group was set up in which a very genuine equality prevailed because those who established the community were for the most part equals. The fundamental rules of the order which were worked out in the first few weeks and months were consequently rules by which equals dealt with one another. When these rules were established, a new member of necessity would come in under them. The original rules, which acquired increasing sanctity, would hardly have been set aside to create a new category of membership unless there was a real need for it and a corresponding demand. Apparently there was none. The Essenes discovered in their own experience both the joy of a brotherhood in which all men are equal and the validity of the principle as well. The theory of equality among men would not have been new to them if they were educated men as most of them undoubtedly were. What would have been new to them would have been the experience of equality in practice. After learning the values of equality in their own experience, they would then have learned to state it as a principle.

It was in their common meals that the Essenes seem to have experienced fellowship most completely. This is not surprising, for the experience is universal. Each of the members of the community knew the others, and mealtime was a period for relaxation and talking. With the Essenes all meals became communal and all had a sacramental quality. The Manual of Discipline says: "Together they shall eat, and together they shall worship, and together they shall counsel. . . . And when they set the table to eat, or the wine to drink, the priest shall stretch out his hand first to pronounce a blessing with the first portion of the bread and the wine."

Another factor that made for a feeling of interdependence and community was the strict rule that all things were to be held in common. The Manual of Discipline says: "All who have offered themselves for [God's] truth shall bring all their knowledge and strength and wealth into the community of God, to purify their knowledge in the truth of God's statutes, and to distribute their strength according to the perfection of his ways, and all their property according to his righteous counsel." Theirs was not a simple "share-the-wealth" program; they created a community in which not only material goods, but also "knowledge" and "strength," were shared. Apparently the three were regarded as of equal importance to the community.

Were there women in the order? The evidence we have is conflicting and a conclusive answer is impossible. The three ancient authorities, Josephus, Philo and Pliny, agree that the Essenes excluded women from the order as a matter of principle, yet Josephus says there is a sect among the Essenes that permits marriage. The Damascus Document includes several references to women and children, which obviously imply the presence of women. The same is true of the "Two Column" fragment. Archeologists report that the bones of women were found in some of the graves at Khirbet Qumran. A possible solution is that women were originally a part of the order, but that later celibacy was established.

In the later period which Josephus and Philo knew and about which they wrote so vividly, life in the order seems to have been well-regularized and to have attained a very high quality. Josephus wrote:

"After this every one of them are sent away by their curator to exercise some of those arts wherein they are skilled, in which they labour with great diligence till the fifth hour; after which they assemble themselves again into one place. And when they have clothed themselves in white loincloths, they then bathe their bodies in cold water. . . . They quietly set themselves down, upon which the baker lays them loaves in order. The cook also brings a single plate of one sort of food and sets it before every one of them. But a priest says grace before, and it is unlawful for anyone to taste of the food before grace is said. The same priest, when he hath dined, says grace again after meat. And when they begin, and when they end, they praise God as he that bestows their food upon them, after which they lay aside their garments [their white garments] and betake themselves to their labours until the evening. Then they return home to supper after the same manner, and if there be any stranger, they sit down with them."

There is no question concerning the commanding ideal that possessed them. Their vision of what men ought to be and what they ought to do made the Essenes what they were. They are important in their own right, quite apart from any connection there may be between their teachings and practices and those of Christianity. The following paragraph from the Manual of Discipline summarizes their attitude as well as anything we possess:

"But in a spirit of true counsel for the ways of a man all his iniquities will be atoned, so that he will look at the light of life, and in a holy spirit he will be united in his truth; and he will be cleansed from all his iniquities; and in an upright and humble spirit his sin will be atoned, and in the submission of his soul to all the statutes of God his flesh will be cleansed, that he may be sprinkled with water for impurity and sanctify himself with water of cleanness. And he will establish his steps, to walk perfectly in all the ways of God, as he commanded for the appointed times of his testimonies, and not to turn aside to right or left, and not to transgress against one of all his words. Then he will be accepted by pleasing atonements before God; and this will be for him a covenant of eternal community."

8

Piety and Politics

Alexander Jannaeus lived for ten years following the night in 88 B.C. when he displayed his vengeance toward the Pharisees and other pietists in Jerusalem. During those years he was almost constantly waging war. At first he was involved in a conflict with the king of Syria and Aretas of Arabia. The remainder of his reign was given to an attempt to subdue the region just east of the Jordan. He took in succession Dion, Heshbon, Pella, Gerasa and Gamala. Returning to Jerusalem, he received a conqueror's welcome. He was engaged in the siege of Ragaba, another Trans-Jordanian town, when he was killed in 78 B.C.

If the evidence of the archeologists is correct in indicating that the year 110 B.C., or thereabouts, was the date of the founding of the Qumran colony, thirty years separated the origin of the Essene movement and the end of the reign of Alexander Jannaeus. These years were pivotal in their history. We have no details of these thirty years, except for the scraps of information about the Teacher of Righteousness, the Wicked Priest and the Man of the Lie found in the Scroll literature. We have, however, a great body of indirect information.

As the persecution of the Pharisees increased under Alexander

Jannaeus, Qumran would have become even more precious to them. They had left Jerusalem in order to follow the Law of the Lord in the manner they thought was right. They also desired to get away from the jibes of their enemies, among whom the Pharisees were certainly included. All this they had already achieved. During the reign of Jannaeus, however, they would have begun to look upon their community at Qumran as a haven of refuge from far greater suffering than they themselves endured. As the most devout of all the sons of Israel, they could hardly have expected to fare better than the Pharisees, who seem to have borne the full brunt of Jannaeus' fury. How precious Qumran must have seemed as they heard of the events taking place in Jerusalem in this period!

One scholar has guessed that Alexander Jannaeus actually came to Qumran, but it is a surmise only, for the evidence in support of it is very slender. Nevertheless, the increasing sense of insecurity that the Essenes felt during his reign, their anxiety that he might at any time descend upon them, would have been very real. But a few miles up the Jordan from their desert home he was engaged in subjugating the towns east of the Jordan. When might he not turn upon them?

Many of the Dead Sea Scroll Psalms describe this state of affairs. Psalm XI is typical. It may be a psalm of the Teacher of Righteousness or it may have been intended to describe his feelings. As such, the words must have seemed both real and comforting to the refugees from the Lion of Wrath.

I thank thee, O Lord, because thou hast sustained me with thy strength and hast shed abroad thy Holy Spirit in me;
I shall not be moved.
Thou hast strengthened me in the face of the battles of wickedness;
in all the ruin they wrought thou didst not turn in dismay from thy covenant.
Thou hast made me like a strong tower,
like a high wall;
thou hast established my building on a rock,
with eternal bases as my foundation,
and all my walls as a tested wall
that will not be shaken.

> For the lying lips shall be dumb;
> for all who attack me for judgment thou wilt condemn,
> separating by me the righteous from the wicked.
> For thou knowest every purpose of action
> and perceivest every answer of the tongue.
> Thou hast established my heart in thy teachings and in thy truth,
> to direct my steps to the paths of righteousness,
> that I might walk before thee in the region of life,
> to the path of glory and peace.

The psalmist praises the Lord for giving him the strength to hold to the covenant in the face of wickedness. He refers to his trials before going to Qumran, but apparently a similar state of affairs existed at the time of his writing. Consequently, the Lord is still his strong tower and high wall. Even now, the psalmist cannot be shaken. The determination to hold on through possible future danger is unmistakable. The covenant of the Lord still stands. The Lord has not turned away despite the ruin wrought by the legions of wickedness. The psalmist assures himself and all others who will heed his words that it is still worth while to keep the Lord's covenant.

Psalm III, reflecting the same circumstances, may also have been composed by or in behalf of the Teacher of Righteousness. It mirrors the experience any member of the Essene colony might have had before going to Qumran. The warlike overtones suggest the reign of Jannaeus rather than the reign of his father Hyrcanus. The psalm is a song of thanksgiving to God for strength given through the covenant. This enabled the psalmist to escape "the snares of the pit" and the "oppressors who sought [his] life."

> I thank thee, O Lord,
> Because thou hast put my soul in the bundle of life; . . .
> Though my heart melted like water,
> My soul took hold of thy covenant.
> The net they spread for me caught their own feet;
> They fell into the traps they had hid for my soul.
> But my foot stands on level ground;
> In the assembly I will bless thy name.

Then came the death of Alexander Jannaeus. His widow Alexandra succeeded him. Completely reversing her husband's policies, she opened the prison doors and freed all of Jannaeus' political enemies. She appointed her eldest son as high priest, ousted the Sadducees from political control and threw her lot with the Pharisees. Almost overnight the complexion of Jerusalem was completely changed.

Alexandra's support of the Pharisees may have been a matter of conviction or policy, or perhaps something of both. Josephus says Jannaeus advised it on his deathbed. In any case, she brought the Pharisees back into favor and authority. Her brother, Simon Ben Shetach, a member of the group and apparently her confidant, may well be the key to her action. The fact that Alexandra's brother was a Pharisee shows the tangled personal relationships of the Hasmonean period when the conflicts between the Pharisees and the Sadducees constantly crossed family, party and sectarian lines. It is difficult for us to appreciate how closely the interests of one group were interwoven with the other.

Alexandra showed her sympathy for the Pharisees by increasing the authority of the Jerusalem Council which doubtless had been more Saducaic than Pharisaic. She created a new group of scholars in the Law, the scribes, of whom Israel was to hear much thereafter. The refugees who had fled in terror from the barbarity by which Jannaeus maintained himself in power now streamed back to their capital city. The Pharisees afterward were to look upon the reign of Alexandra as one of the noblest periods in Israel's history. The Pharisaic tradition regarding the reign of Alexandra reads:

"Under Simon Ben Shetach and Queen Salome [Alexandra] rain fell on the eve of the Sabbath, so that the grains of wheat were as large as kidneys, the barley as large as olives, and the lentils like golden denarii; the scribes gathered such corns and preserved specimens of them in order to show future generations what sin entails."

Alexandra reigned for nine years from 78 to 69 B.C. Not since the early days of John Hyrcanus, two generations before, had the Law been so widely respected and so thoroughly enforced, nor had the devout and pious among the Jews been so joyful. They were free to follow the covenant of the Lord and they were free to impose it upon the whole nation. They began, for

the first time since the reign of John Hyrcanus, to dream of a
free Israel living as the elect of God in accordance with his Law.

The Essenes at this juncture must have faced the question of
whether they should remain loyal to the order and continue on in
the desert or return to Jerusalem to help lead all Israel back
to the covenant. Surely this represented a real crisis in their
internal development. They would not only have had to think
through the basic premises of their separate existence, but they
would also have had to resolve the whole matter of withdrawal
from, or intervention in, the political affairs of men.

When the old Torah was rigidly enforced, the Sadducees, the
members of the ancient nobility and the warriors who had fought
with Alexander Jannaeus, became increasingly uncomfortable,
resentful and restless. Furthermore, piety and vindictiveness probably were not separated. The Pharisees enforced their Judaizing
principles with a severity that was perhaps not quite all piety,
although they could account for their measure by appealing to
the requirements of the Mosaic Law. Their zeal served to quicken
the old war party's yearning for power. It began to make plans
and when Queen Alexandra died, it was ready.

Alexander Jannaeus and Alexandra had two sons, Hyrcanus
II, whom his mother had made high priest, and Aristobulus II,
who, thirsting for power and eager to be king, became a willing
tool of the Sadducees and the old war party of Alexander Jannaeus. The opposing forces, led by the two brothers, met in
battle "near Jericho" in 68 B.C., and Hyrcanus II was decisively
defeated.

What was the effect of this succession of events on the Essenes
at Qumran? Their sympathies would certainly have been with
the Pharisees and Hyrcanus II. Some of them may actually have
fought with him against Aristobulus II, although Josephus says
that the Essenes were pacifists, an observation which may refer to
a later period when they seem to have become convinced that
all fighting was useless.

Thus the struggle for power between Alexandra's two sons
necessitated a decision among the Essenes. When the Sadducaic
nobility prepared to overthrow the Pharisaic government, the

Essenes would have had to determine whether to support the Pharisees who were their kindred spirits, or whether by refusing to help to offer indirectly comfort to their old enemies. When the battle was fought "near Jericho" the Essenes may have taken an active part. In any case, they could not have been unaffected by it.

Hyrcanus II was defeated, but he was not routed. He continued the struggle for the kingship as best he could. Consequently, the civil war dragged on, a senseless internal struggle for power which was characterized by religious fanaticism. Always present was the question of the degree to which Law was to be followed. A foreign power, seeing the Jews at war with one another, now intervened. In the hope of appropriating control of Palestine for himself, Antipater the Idumean threw his weight with Hyrcanus II, perhaps at the latter's urging, with the result that Aristobulus II was routed.

At this juncture, however, Rome stepped into the affairs of Israel and the little, though bloody, contests for power within the nation were thereafter completely inundated in her sudden rise to power. A Roman general, representing Pompey, now moved forward. Both Aristobulus II and Hyrcanus II sent delegations to curry his favor and win his support. Aristobulus' plea was apparently the more effective, for Rome gave her support to him. With so impressive an ally behind him, Aristobulus now fell upon his brother Hyrcanus and dealt him a crushing defeat. This made him master of all Judea and put the Sadducees in power again.

Pompey now appeared at Damascus. Aristobulus and Hyrcanus and also a third group of Jews, we are told, made their pleas for his support. Aristobulus and Hyrcanus wanted the crown and the high priesthood, but the third group asked that these offices be given to neither of the two contenders. The two offices should be divided, they said. It was their belief that it would be better for Israel and for Rome if Pompey were to appoint a high priest for the Temple and to retain the reins of government himself.

What this third group wanted is obvious in the light of the

previous hundred and fifty years of Jewish history. They wanted an end of priest-kings, whose hands, stained with the blood of their own people, offered sacrifices at the high altar. They hoped for an end of internecine strife and fratricidal warfare which had decimated Israel for more than a century. They longed for a restoration of the high priesthood under a Roman governor. This, they believed, would bring peace to their unhappy land and enable Israel once more to follow the Law of the Lord. They wanted, in short, a restoration of the conditions which had prevailed under the Ptolemies and Antiochus the Great nearly two hundred years before. Then the Children of Israel, under the rule of a foreign power, lived at peace with one another and kept the covenant of the Lord.

How earnestly the most pious in Israel yearned to see the Law established, even if under a foreign overlord, may be seen in the Psalms of Solomon, part of the literature of the pseudepigrapha. We know that this point of view was congenial to the Essenes, for the fragments of the Psalms of Solomon were found at Qumran. The Psalms give a vivid account of the hatred which pious Jews felt toward the Hasmonean priest-kings. A characteristic passage reads:

"God laid bare their sins in the sight of the sun; all the earth hath learned the righteous judgments of God. . . . The holy things of God they took for spoil; and there was no inheritor to deliver out of their hand. They went up to the altar of the Lord when they were full of all uncleanness; yea, even in their separation they polluted the sacrifices, eating them like profane meats. They left not a sin undone, wherein they offended not above the heathen. For this cause did God mingle for them a spirit of error, he made them to drink of the cup of unmixed wine until they were drunken. He brought him that is from the utmost part of the earth, whose stroke is might; he decreed war against Jerusalem and her land. The princes of the land met him with joy; they said unto him, Blessed is thy path! come ye, enter in with peace. They made the rough paths even before their entering in, they opened the gates that led into Jerusalem, her walls they crowned with garlands. He entered in, as a father entereth into

his sons' house, in peace. He established his feet and made them
very firm. He occupied her strongholds, yea, and the wall of
Jerusalem. For God led him in safety, because of their blindness.
He cut off their princes and every wise councillor; he poured
out the blood of the dwellers in Jerusalem like the water of
uncleanness, he carried away their sons and their daughters
whom they had begotten in their defilement. They had done
according to their uncleanness, even as their fathers did, they
polluted Jerusalem and the things that had been dedicated unto
the name of God."

Whence came this delegation to Pompey and who were the
men that formed it? Although we do not know for certain, we
may be sure that they were not Sadducees, for the Sadducees
favored Aristobulus II. We may be equally sure they were not
Pharisees, for the Pharisees favored Hyracanus II. We are no
less certain that the point of view they adopted and the arguments they advanced are entirely consistent with the position
of the Essenes on such matters. If the men of Qumran did not
themselves make up the embassy, perhaps their more practical-
minded associates at Jerusalem did. This is speculation, not fact,
but it is the kind of surmise that fits into all that we do know
and contradicts nothing about which we are certain.

If the surmise is correct, it means that, after a brief interval,
the old idea of eschewing political power reasserted itself at
Qumran, granting, of course, that it had first to be given up.
The use of political power may never have been considered
by them at all. Whatever we conclude as to this particular detail, we know that by the time Pompey entered Damascus and
the high priesthood had changed hands between Aristobulus and
Hyrcanus three times, the Essenes were insisting again that Israel
must cease to look for her redemption through political power.
They now hoped for a true and worthy high priest at the Temple
in Jerusalem and an Israel dwelling under the Mosaic Law beneath the civil arm of Rome. They may once more have been
drawn into the internecine wars of the Jews, but they never again
looked for a Jewish king on the throne of David. Now they began
to think more and more of the coming of the Lord's anointed,

the Messiah, and for the redemption of Israel through those who kept his covenant.

None of the Jewish delegations that came to Pompey at Damascus was successful. Having heard all three, he took the case under advisement. This meant that things remained as they were for the moment, with Aristobulus in the office of high priest and nominally "king" while the old priestly Sadducean party continued to enjoy a supremacy at Jerusalem which they had not had since the time of Alexander Jannaeus. Aristobulus, however, foolishly concluding that he did not need the backing of Rome to keep himself in power, decided to resist. The result was inevitable. Pompey marched on Jerusalem. Hyrcanus and the Pharisees opened the gates of the city to him. Thereupon Aristobulus and his followers retreated to the Temple where they withstood the siege successfully for a time. In the end, of course, Pompey breached the walls, and according to Josephus twelve thousand Jews were massacred before the city was subdued. It was on this occasion that Pompey entered the Holy of Holies in the Temple, a prerogative of the high priest alone and his but once a year. Pompey was amazed to find it empty. His brashness may have satisfied his curiosity, but in Jewish eyes it was a desecration which both of the contending parties at Jerusalem joined in denouncing.

Pompey installed Hyrcanus II as high priest, and sent Aristobulus off to Rome as one of the exhibits in his triumphal procession, after the manner of victorious Roman generals in those days. Now the Pharisees were back in power again after an interval of only six years. The "peace party" in Jerusalem, made up of Pharisees and perhaps Essenes too, had succeeded better than they had wanted to do. They had desired political and religious power over the Jewish people under the strong arm of Rome in order that the old Mosaic Law might be held in proper honor. Few of them could have desired what they had helped to bring about, namely, the end of Jewish national independence. Yet after Pompey took Jerusalem in 63 B.C. the Jews were never politically independent again.

There was peace among the Jews for a period of six years following Pompey's conquest. We may suppose that this, like the

situation during the reign of Alexandra, was a difficult time at
the Essene Community Center. With the Pharisees in power, the
Law would be strictly enforced. Again, as under Alexandra, life
in the desert would no longer have seemed necessary. Now
again it was possible to follow the Law in all its literalness even
while living in Jerusalem. Consequently, unless there are important factors at play here which we do not grasp, we are led
to conclude that the first decade after Pompey took Jerusalem
was another period in which serious problems were faced by the
Essenes at Qumran.

The Sadducees and the old warrior nobles, however, still
yearned both for the power they themselves once had had and
for political independence for their nation. So doubtless did
some of those who had formerly supported Hyrcanus II. In the
years from 57 to 52 B.C., the Jews rebelled no less than four times.
On each occasion it was the old war party that led the revolt.
The first rebellion was initiated by a son of Aristobulus II. Rome
easily put it down but as a result Hyrcanus was deprived of what
little political power had been left to him in his role of ethnarch
in spite of the fact that Hyrcanus wanted no part of the uprising.
Now Hyrcanus was high priest only, Palestine in effect became
a part of Syria, and its government was given to the Roman governor of Syria. The remaining three revolts were also easily put
down by Rome. Thereafter Palestine enjoyed another decade
or more of peace. Meanwhile, the Pharisees continued in power
and the old Mosaic Law held the central place in Jewish culture
and religion.

Then began the great period of civil war in Rome, which involved ultimately the whole Mediterranean world. Julius Caesar
crossed the Rubicon in 49 B.C. and for twenty years thereafter
Roman fought Roman for control of the empire. Life in Palestine
was for the most part unaffected by these titanic events. Caesar
confirmed Hyrcanus II as hereditary high priest, granted him
Roman citizenship and restored him to the office of ethnarch of
Judea.

The old party divisions, loyalties and hatreds in Israel, meanwhile, continued on as intense as before. Now it was Antigonus,

son of Aristobulus II, around whom the old aristocrats, the Sadducees, the war party and the nationalists rallied. Meanwhile Herod ruled Palestine while Caesar, Cassius and Mark Antony in succession represented the final authority of Rome. Finally in 41 B.C. Rome's leaders had become so involved with each other in the struggle for power that Anigonus and his party decided the time had come to strike. With the backing of Parthia, Rome's great rival in the east, they seized Hyrcanus II and drove out Herod. Once again the old priestly war party was back in control at Jerusalem with Antigonus installed as high priest, and claiming the title of king as well. Apparently Antigonus' rebellion was at least in part a nationalist uprising, because he was able to enlist the support of religiously fanatical Jews in Galilee.

Now Herod having secured the title "King of the Jews" from Rome, returned and took up the struggle with Antigonus. He defeated the forces of Antigonus in Galilee after a strenuous campaign among the hills and caves of that region. The next year, backed by two Roman legions, Herod pushed on into Judea. In the attempt to subdue it, he too fought a battle "near Jericho." Again the coincidence is arresting. This was the year 38 B.C., about the time we know the Qumran Community Center to have been abandoned. The next year, the spring of 37 B.C., Herod laid siege to Jerusalem. The old priestly war party were the defenders once more. It is incredible that this should have happened yet again. As before, the defenders fought with fanaticism. There was new carnage; the streets again ran red with the blood of the Jewish people. Both the Romans and Herod's forces simply cut the Jewish people down like ripened grain. Again it was the Pharisees who opened the gates of the city to the besiegers.

Herod fully realized the sacredness of the Temple to the Jews of all parties, and he was able to prevent any desecration of it. In order to avoid further trouble from the Aristobulus line he executed Antigonus. He also executed forty-five members of the old Jewish nobility who had been supporters of Antigonus and who with him had fomented rebellion. It was the end of the political power of the Sadduccees.

Herod was a proselyte and in consequence could not occupy

the office of high priest. He could not install the aged Hyrcanus II in the office, for Antigonus had cut off his ears, which under Jewish Law made him ineligible. In place of Hyrcanus, Herod appointed a Jew from Babylon, while retaining most of the civil power himself. This left the Pharisees still in the ascendancy, although their power was now entirely confined to religious and cultural matters.

Such was the political scene in Judea during the first period of occupancy of the Community Center of the Essenes at Qumran. Such were the turbulent times in which they lived, the clash of empires, the invincible power of Rome coupled with her inability to govern herself. As Jew had fought Jew for supremacy at Jerusalem so Roman now fought Roman for supremacy all over the Mediterranean world.

In addition to the struggle for power at Rome and her effort to control Asia Minor, we have also to remember the continuing ambition of Syria, Egypt and other Eastern empires to control Palestine. In this period Syria, Egypt, Parthia, Idumea and Nabatea are contending with one another for supremacy while Rome is engaged in sweeping them all into her empire and keeping them there. The Essenes lived in a time and place when a three-level contest for power was in process. In fact, it was a four-level affair if Rome's conquest of the East is to be included. There was the contest for power at Rome itself; there was the contest among the lesser Eastern monarchs for the control of Asia Minor, which involved standing in with whoever happened to be in power at Rome; and there was the contest for the high priesthood at Jerusalem which involved standing in with whomever Rome happened to designate as governor of Syria.

Trying to look upon the scene from the relatively detached position of the Essenes, we see the Pharisees in control of the affairs of Israel almost throughout this entire period. There was a stretch of six years following the death of Alexandra when the Sadducees were in control. There was another stretch of four years from 41 to 37 B.C. during which the old war party again raised the standard of revolt. Apart from these two brief periods, however, both of which ended with a siege of Jerusalem by Rome and the slaughter of thousands of Jews, the Pharisees were in control the entire time.

We have assumed that differences among the Pharisees resulted in the first exodus to Qumran. These differences were minor as compared with the differences between the Pharisees and Sadducees. In the struggles between these two latter groups, the sympathies of the Essenes must always have been with the Pharisees, even if they did not actively enter into the contests for power in which these antagonists were almost constantly locked. As a result, throughout this period the Essenes were always faced with the problem of involvement versus withdrawal. They had had no problem on this score down to the death of Alexander Jannaeus. With Pharisees in power and the old Torah re-established in Jerusalem, however, they were confronted by a very real issue, particularly when the political power of the Pharisees was in jeopardy. As had been the case with the Hasidim, a hundred years before, they were forced constantly to decide whether to maintain their position of withdrawal or whether actively to support the policies in Jerusalem in which they deeply believed.

Again and again the Essenes must have had to decide. We are left with no clue as to what decision they reached unless the story of the third delegation that came to Pompey at Damascus is an Essene story. We can, however, be certain of their emotional if not of their political involvement. Believing as they did in Israel as the Lord's chosen people, believing in his covenant with his people, and the requirement that they keep their part of it by following the Law, they must always have rejoiced to see Pharisees in power in Jerusalem, even as they had concluded in the reign of Alexander Jannaeus that the covenant was broken forever and that only they, the remnant in the desert, could ever redeem it. How deeply the Essene colony was involved in spite of their attempt to remain apart in the desert, we shall now try to discover from such evidence as is available.

9

THE COMMUNITY CENTER IS ABANDONED

Sometime about twenty-five years after the coming of Pompey the Essenes abandoned their enterprise at the Wadi Qumran. The movement itself was not given up for they returned to Qumran about two generations later. Coins, debris and other archeological data point to A.D. 6, the beginning of the Christian Era, as the date of the reoccupancy of Qumran by the Essenes. The work of Père Roland DeVaux and G. Lankester Harding has established these matters for us. The year 31 B.C. is the final possible date of the first period of the Qumran settlement. There was an earthquake in Palestine in that year and a fault occurred in the ground under the Essene Community Center itself. It is quite clear that the site was not occupied for many years afterward.

Coins found in the course of the excavations indicate that the Essenes may have abandoned their Community Center as much as six or eight years before the earthquake. While this evidence is not conclusive, it does indicate that if the site was occupied during the last six or eight years before the earthquake there was very little activity there as compared with that of former years.

Why did the Essenes abandon the enterprise at Qumran after

some seventy-five years? Did they regard the earthquake as an evidence that the wrath of God was visited upon them for a supposed sin? Did they flee in terror for their lives? Or are the archeologists right in saying that the Qumran Community Center had already been abandoned before the earthquake came?

Charles T. Fritsch points to the fact that Herod the Great had by this time built his summer pleasure palace at Jericho, less than seven miles from Qumran. He reasons that the two colonies would have been quite uncongenial. But we have no hint as to whether Herod drove the Essenes out, whether they quit in disgust at the intrusion of so alien a spirit, or whether Herod's presence at Jericho had anything at all to do with their giving up the enterprise. Herod would not have troubled himself with a little group of desert dwellers watching for the coming of the last days, it would seem, unless they were revolutionary, a surmise that is precluded by their increasing pacifism. Furthermore, why would Herod's court, though filled with pleasure-lovers, have greatly troubled the Essenes, removed as they were by some seven miles of burning desert hardpan?

Another question, when answered adequately, explains the exodus from Qumran. This question is not why the Essenes left Qumran, but rather why the Qumran Community continued as long as it did? What principle of cohesion, what secret strength, what human ideal was so compelling that life in the desert seemed worth while to the Essenes for fifty years after the Pharisees were restored to power and the Law was made supreme in Israel once more? If the community was celibate during this time, as seems probable, the Essenes would have had not only to maintain their membership without much defection, but they would also constantly have had to attract recruits. At times this must have been difficult.

Consider, for example, the effect of the death of the Teacher of Righteousness on the Essene movement. Must not the colony have experienced a decided slump immediately afterward? The members must have felt hopeless, lost and confounded. Far from the corruptions of men, they had sought under his leadership to follow the Law of the Lord and to meditate in it day and night. Indeed, they had taken this description of the blessed man in Psalm I of our Old Testament literally, so literally that in every group of ten, one member was constantly reading the ancient Scriptures of Israel. When Yahweh permitted their leader to be taken from them, what hope or what mission was left for them? Why carry on and for what purpose?

If we are right in assuming any such sense of despair on the part of the Essenes, obviously they overcame it, for the colony at Qumran continued on for some fifty years afterward. The memory of the Teacher of Righteousness shortly became central for the movement, and he seems in their writings to have been held in increasing reverence. Although the Damascus Document says merely that "God . . . raised for them a teacher of righteousness," the Habakkuk Commentary violently denounces the persecution of the Teacher of Righteousness by the Wicked Priest. The psalm fragments which mention the Teacher of Righteousness are equally strong.

The barbarity of Alexander Jannaeus undoubtedly accounts for the strength of the Essene movement during the fifteen or more years he ruled Israel. This in part accounts for the fact that the movement continued to be strong even after the death of the Teacher of Righteousness. The real problem, as we have seen, came for the first time during the reign of Queen Alexandra, when the Pharisees were restored to political power in Jerusalem. During that period there must have been an intense struggle within the Essene colony over the question of withdrawal from, or participation in, the struggle for power at Jerusalem. The counterpart of that struggle during the benign rule of Queen Alexandra was the issue of loyalty or backsliding.

Theological purists who separate themselves from the rest of society and voluntarily take hardship upon themselves, thrive upon adversity. When their enemies are in power, the separatist group prospers. Separatism derives its strength from those whom it opposes. On the contrary such a group is robbed of much of its strength when its enemies are discomfitted and the high standards it desires to attain become possible of achievement within, rather than apart from, society as a whole.

Consequently, we can assume that some of the Essenes, feeling that the Qumran enterprise was no longer worth while, gladly returned to Jerusalem to enjoy the political power which had now come into the hands of the Pharisees. Perhaps it was at that time that the very stern strictures against those who left the Essene order were instituted.

We have seen in the Manual of Discipline the curses the Essenes heaped upon those who had fallen away. They were uttered by the priests and the Levites when the initiate was admitted to the Essene order or "passing over into the covenant," as the Essenes put it. In the course of these ceremonies, equally vehement curses were uttered against the "sons of Belial" who never entered the covenant at all. These curses were obviously intended further to strengthen the neophyte in his resolve to separate himself from the world. The curse of the Essenes against all Israelites who did not join them, as contained in the Manual of Discipline, reads:

"Accursed may you be in all your wicked, guilty works; may God make you a horror through all those that wreak vengeance and send after you destruction through all those that pay recompense; accursed may you be without mercy according to the darkness of your works, and may you suffer wrath in the deep darkness of eternal fire. May God not be gracious to you when you call, and may he not pardon, forgiving your iniquities; may he lift up his angry countenance for vengeance upon you, and may there be no peace for you at the mouth of all those that hold enmity!"

These curses explain two points. First, they show the length to which the Essenes went in their attempt to create a virtually indissoluble membership. The growth of this idea is seen by comparing the fierce vituperation on backsliding in the passages in the Manual of Discipline with those in the Damascus Document. The Damascus Document is more in the mood of the Old Testament in which all Israel is chided for backsliding. Hosea compared backsliders to a backsliding heifer.

The Damascus Document reads:

"The faithless are those that backslide from the way. . . . Those who followed the Man of Scoffing and turned aside from the pathways of righteousness . . . they searched out smooth things and condemned the just, and caused others to transgress the covenant and to break the ordinance, and gathered against the soul of the righteous man . . . and the wrath of God was kindled against their congregation so as to make desolate all their multitude; and their works are as impurity before Him."

Secondly, the curses show how dire was the necessity for setting every obstacle in the way of those who, finding the rigors of life in the desert too much for them, wanted to return to the comforts of Jerusalem; those who felt, as a matter of conviction, that with the Pharisees in power in Jerusalem and the old Torah strictly enforced once more, there was no point in maintaining the Qumran community any longer; and those who felt called upon, as a matter of conscience, to return to Jerusalem to give their strength to the Pharisees who were always in more or less danger of losing control to the Sadducees again. The Essenes, in their effort to hold the Qumran community together, steadily moved toward classing these groups as backsliders.

How otherwise are we to explain the increasing ferocity of the Essene curses on backsliding? How otherwise are we to explain the shift from their condemning a particular group of backsliders (those who followed the Man of Scoffing) to all backsliders from the movement, regardless of their reasons for leaving Qumran? We should expect the curses to be fiercest on the part of those who suffered the most—namely, those who lived through the reign of Alexander Jannaeus. We find, instead, that they are fiercest of all in the Manual of Discipline, which represents a late period in the development of the Essene movement.

Besides normal human frailty and the other motives that led to backsliding, another factor tended in that direction. Because they were millennialists and looked for the coming of the Messiah, as did many people in Israel in the first century B.C., they believed that the end of days was not far off.

The Essenes had gone into the wilderness to prepare the way of the Lord, in accordance with prophecies of the end of days found in Daniel and Enoch and other apocalyptic literature. The

Essenes were thoroughly convinced that the end was near. Why, they must have wondered after a time, was the end so long delayed?

We know from their own writings that this became a serious problem for the covenantors of Qumran. The Commentary on Habakkuk 2:3, reads: *"For still the vision is for an appointed time: it hastens to the period and does not lie."* This means that the last period extends over and above all that the prophets said. To the further words of Habakkuk, *"If it tarries, wait for it, for it will surely come: it will not delay,"* the commentator adds: "This means the men of truth, the doers of the Law, whose hands do not grow slack from the service of the truth, when the last period is stretched out over them. For all the periods of God will come to their fixed term as he decreed for them in the mysteries of his wisdom." The eschatalogy here is unmistakable. The end of days is expected, and the "doers of the law" and those who follow "the service of the truth" have only to hold fast until the final day comes.

Again the Habakkuk Commentary reads: "And truly the saying refers to those who will act treacherously at the end of days; that is those who are ruthless against the covenant, who do not believe when they hear all the things that are coming upon the last generation. . . . And God told Habakkuk to write the things that were to come upon the last generation." This obviously means the time in which the commentator is writing, for he adds, "But the consummation of the period he did not make known to him. . . . God will set the judgment in the midst of many peoples . . . and in their midst will condemn it and punish it with fire of brimstone." For this writer the judgment day clearly is at hand.

The twofold purpose of all apocalyptic literature can be discerned here. On the one hand, the faithful are to believe that God will intervene to destroy the wicked who are so numerous and who have gained such complete control of the world that to struggle against them seems useless. On the other hand, the faithful are also to believe that they themselves must be faithful in following the way of righteousness until the end of days has come. The difficulty in the apocalyptic point of view is that the end never comes.

What of the man who read the Habakkuk Commentary a generation or more after it was written? What did he think? How did he answer the question why the promised day of the Lord was so long delayed? There could only have been the answer Israel had been giving for hundreds of years. The prophets had explained that the Law had not been followed and that the Lord was angry with his people.

In defending themselves against their critics within the movement, who desired to return to Jerusalem, and those without, who never favored the withdrawal to Qumran, the Essenes worked out a doctrine by which they accounted for and justified their separate identity. They came to think of themselves as people of "the way." They believed that God would execute judgment upon all who despised him and this to the Essenes included just about all Israel. But, they concluded, God would again save a remnant of his people who were willing to keep the covenant, even as he had saved a remnant in the days of the prophets. Knowing themselves to be "guilty men," they nevertheless came to look upon themselves as that remnant and justified themselves because with a perfect heart they sought the Lord. Yet even this conviction apparently was not enough and the enterprise at Qumran had finally to be given up. We do not know exactly why. Perhaps there was a dwindling of interest until the project was no longer able to sustain itself in the wilderness of Judea. Perhaps there was a small nucleus that remained—a determined few who were still clinging to the old ideal when the Community Center was destroyed in 31 B.C. We may suppose that if the colony had been flourishing at the time of the earthquake, they would have immediately rebuilt the Center. Thus we conclude that the enterprise at Qumran slowly lost momentum, beginning with the reign of Alexandra and continuing through the Roman occupation, until it was finally given up sometime between 40 and 31 B.C.

10

WHERE WAS "THE LAND OF DAMASCUS"?

Of all the questions that arise in connection with the Essenes, none has been more earnestly debated than their whereabouts during the two generations they were not at Qumran. For a time the Dead Sea Scroll scholars thought that the Essenes went to Damascus. This was a natural conjecture, for it explained both the hiatus at Qumran and the statement in the Damascus Document that the people with whom it is concerned went to "the land of Damascus." A closer examination of the Damascus Document, however, does not support this initial assumption.

In the first clear reference to the Damascus sojourn the author writes: "The priests are the captivity of Israel who went forth from the land of Judah, and the Levites are those who joined them." The meaning of the words is unmistakable; the group "went forth from the land of Judah." Now Qumran is in the land of Judah, or at least in the borderland, so that it could be so described. But if the Essenes had gone from so specific and isolated a spot as the Essene Community Center, should we not expect some language other than this? We might rather expect to find that they went forth from the "desert of Judah" or the "wilderness of Judah."

The author, of course, might have said "land of Judah" even though he was thinking of the Qumran Community Center. But there are other points to consider. For example, he speaks of the proper observance of the Law "according to the decision of those who entered the new covenant in the land of Damascus." The Essenes at Qumran already regarded themselves as being under a new covenant, but these words, at least as far as the Damascus group is concerned, seem to indicate that the new covenant was not entered into until they reached Damascus.

The most conclusive evidence, however, is of a different sort. Many passages make it clear that the people of the Damascus Document separated themselves from the rest of Israel because of Israel's apostasy.

In the opening passages the author seems to be relating history. He implies that the group to which he belongs is a remnant of the true Israel, even as the Babylonian exiles had been a remnant of the true Israel hundreds of years before. "God hid his face from Israel and from his Sanctuary when the people forsook him and sinned," he says, "and by way of punishment he gave them to the sword." This statement would apply to the contemporary civil wars as well as to Babylonian times. But God "caused a remnant to remain of Israel," the author continues, "and gave them not up to be consumed. . . . He caused to grow forth from Israel and Aaron a root of cultivation to possess his land."

What does he mean? By "remnant" he obviously refers to the group to whom he is addressing his work—namely, the Essenes. Furthermore, it is clear that in his mind they are the remnant of an Israel that forsook God and sinned, so much so that as a result God hid his face both from the people and the Sanctuary they had dedicated to him. In fact the author thinks of the Essenes as a remnant of an Israel so wicked that God gave the people to the sword. Such an Israel could hardly be the Qumran community we have been describing.

To support his position, he cites a passage from Ezekiel which he applies to his own time. Ezekiel said: "The priests and the Levites and the sons of Zadok who kept charge of my sanctuary when the children of Israel strayed from me . . . they shall stand before me." The author of the Damascus Document then adds: "The priests are they that turned from the impiety of Israel, who went out from the land of Judah and the Levites are they that joined hemselves with them, and the sons of Zadok are the elect of Israel." The last phrase apparently means the entire company of the Essenes, "who went out from the land of Judah." The "elect of Israel" and "sons of Zadok" apparently are names by which the Essenes described themselves.

Later on he refers again to those who went out from the land of Judah: "But God remembered the covenant of the forefathers, and he raised from Aaron men of understanding and from Israel men of wisdom. He caused them to hear and they digged the well . . . the well is the Law, and they that digged it are they that turned from the impiety of Israel, who went out from the land of Judah and sojourned in the land of Damascus."

If the Essenes had spent some seventy-five years at Qumran before going to Damascus, can we say that they left because of the apostasy of their own group? It would explain a separatist group that left the "apostates" at Qumran and withdrew to Damascus, but would not explain the removal of the whole group to Damascus that the archeological evidence indicates. The language the author uses is strong and his meaning in these passages is unmistakable.

A typical passage, in which the faithful are instructed as to their duties, says that they are to "keep away from the unclean wealth of wickedness acquired by vowing and devoting and by appropriating the wealth of the sanctuary; and not to rob the poor of his people, so that widows become their spoil, and they murder the fatherless; and to make a separation between the unclean and the clean, and to make men know the difference between the holy and the common; and to keep the Sabbath day according to its explanation, and the festivals and the day of the fast, according to the decision of those who entered the new covenant in the land of Damascus; to contribute their holy things according to their explanation; to love each his brother as himself; and to hold fast the hand of the poor and the needy and the proselyte; and to seek every one the peace of his brother; for a man shall not trespass against his next of kin; and to keep away from harlots according to the ordinance; to rebuke each his brother according to the commandment, and not to bear a grudge from day to day; and to separate from all uncleannesses according to their ordinances; for a man shall not make abominable his holy spirit, as God separated for them."

This is not the language of a man who had left a community such as that at Qumran. It is instead the language of one who had left Israel because he felt that the people as a whole were guilty of all the things he describes. This conclusion becomes the more inescapable as we catch the feeling and the spirit that animates the Damascus Document as a whole. The conviction increases that this document must have been written by a man who left his native land of Judah because he could not endure the sinfulness of his own people.

If the Essenes did not go to Damascus at the conclusion of the first occupancy of Qumran, where did they go? A few ingenious and determined scholars, among them Roland de Vaux and Robert North, have advanced the theory that "Damascus" in the Damascus Document is not a city, but a region. If we confine ourselves to the document itself, which is the safest and surest evidence we have this theory receives ample support. The author always speaks of the "land of Damascus," phraseology that describes an area rather than a city. But North adduces far more impressive evidence to support the surmise which the words themselves suggest.

In their writings, the Essenes used most proper nouns in an figurative sense. "Kittim," for example, which is generally taken to mean Romans, is a code word and its use is not so much allegory as it is disguise. North, by the same token, suggests that "land of Damascus" means the Nabataean kingdom. The Nabataeans took Damascus in 87 B.C., a fact which has only recently come to light. For the next century or more, they controlled most of the region east of the Jordan, extending from Damascus in the north to the region below their capital city of Petra in the south. North argues that the Nabataean kingdom included all the desolate region around the Dead Sea as well as the fertile area at the mouth of the Jordan.

Gaster adds one further bit of evidence for the symbolic character of "Damascus." He says that the Essenes described their sojourn in the desert as exile in "the wilderness of Damascus" in order to link themselves to a prophecy of Amos. "I will take you into exile beyond Damascus, says the Lord, whose name is the God of hosts," Amos had cried. They used Amos' phraseology purposely, Gaster thinks, thereby dramatizing that their going out into the desert to live was a fulfillment of his prophecy. P. R. Weis suggests their symbolic use of "Damascus" may have come from Zechariah who said, "The word of the Lord is against the land of Hadrach, and will rest upon Damascus," or "Damascus shall be his resting place."

All the details which heretofore did not make very good sense find meaning through this theory. The Damascus Document now becomes what it seems on its surface to be, a document of the Essene sect, written after these purists had withdrawn from Israel and gone out into the desert to prepare the way of the Lord. This, in turn, means that there was no exodus to the city of Damascus before the earthquake of 31 B.C., or at any other time. The exodus of the Damascus Document was from Jerusalem into the wilderness of Judea at the time the Essene colony was established at the Wadi Qumran.

If the Essenes were not in Damascus during the years after the Community Center in the desert was unoccupied, there seems to be only one reasonable alternative: they went to Jerusalem. If, with this in mind, we reread the Damascus Document, language that often seems quite obscure takes on considerably more clarity. If the author is an Essene who knew the Qumran community, certain lines become more meaningful. For example, in speaking of those who dug the well, which is the Law, we see that he is obviously speaking of an event which happened long before to someone else.

One of the puzzling features of the Damascus Document is the ordinances in what we might call the second half. Unlike those in the Manual of Discipline, many do not seem to apply to the

Qumran situation, but rather appear to be civil ordinances designed for an urban people. When we recall that John Hyrcanus repealed the ordinances which had been set up by the Pharisees during the early years of his rule, we discover, perhaps, the origin of the minute regulations found in the second half of the Damascus Document and also the great concern for carrying them out which the document exhibits. Is this not precisely what a clique among the Pharisees, who were so strict that they ultimately withdrew into the desert, would have done? If these ordinances are a collection of rules copied by a scribe, perhaps ignorant of their origin, onto the same scroll with the "historical" part of the Damascus Document, we have a satisfactory explanation.

The difficulties the Essenes would have encountered in trying to reproduce the Qumran pattern at Jerusalem must have been great. We have seen the extent to which the isolation of the Essenes was responsible for welding them into a social unit marked by clear boundaries of inclusion and exclusion, and by equally clear rules of conduct. These must have been men extraordinarily imbued with loyalty to the convictions they held, for the group to have survived during this period. It had to persist for two generations in urban surroundings. During those years most of the men who had known the desert colony would have died, and the leadership of the group would have fallen to younger men, who had perhaps been members of the Qumran community while still in their twenties or thirties, or who, perhaps had never been members of the wilderness community at all. If Josephus is right when he says that the Essenes had community centers in every city, this may have been the time when these centers were developed.

There is another very important aspect of Essene thought that undoubtedly played its part in sustaining the movement as a separate entity during the period that Qumran was unoccupied. By the time the wilderness venture was given up, the Essenes possessed an overarching sense of their own destiny and the role they were to play in the cosmic scheme of things. Originally they had thought of themselves as a remnant of the true Israel. They and they alone were the keepers of the Lord's covenant with his chosen people. This conception was put to the test, as we have seen, when Queen Alexandra restored the Pharisees to power. The dilemma the Essenes faced at that time surely contributed to the development of their thought about themselves. They had either to find a new reason for being, or to return to Jerusalem as many of their members undoubtedly desired to do. Their doctrine of the new covenant was either the direct result of this dilemma, or great impetus was lent to it thereby.

The idea of a new covenant to replace or to reinstitute the original compact between Yahweh and Israel was not an invention of the Essenes. They found it in Ezekiel. Gradually, we may suppose, as they came to look upon themselves as the true remnant, they began to think of themselves as the inheritors of the old covenant, now broken and largely ignored by the children of Israel. The Essenes slowly evolved the idea in the process of achieving their own sense of selfhood. As they met the arguments of their members who wanted to return to Jerusalem after the rule of the Pharisees was restored; as they wrestled with the problem of why the end of days did not come; as they reached for an explanation of the fact that Yahweh seemed to show so little concern for the sufferings of Israel—as they strove to make their peace with each of these questions all at the same time, they gradually came to think of themselves as under a new covenant which had now replaced the old one.

The Essene covenant was not, however, a replacement of the original pact God had made with the Children of Israel in the days of Moses. As the Essenes thought of it their covenant was a reaffirmation of the ancient agreement made between Yahweh and his chosen people long before. It was not a "New Covenant" or "New Testament" (an equally good translation) in the Christian sense of a replacement, but rather the old covenant that the Children of Israel had virtually abandoned, taken up and perpetuated by a loyal remnant of the sons of Abraham.

With the Essene belief in a new covenant went the yet more bold idea that they were also the new Israel. They came to the conviction that their people had forfeited the right to look upon themselves as God's elect. That privilege, they believed, had now passed to themselves, to those who were members of the Qumran community. That the Essenes reached such a conception of their movement may be seen in the Manual of Discipline and the Damascus Document. Although these ideas may have come in the later period, they are more likely to have come earlier in the days when they were called upon by their enemies to justify their separate existence at Qumran.

Out of the Essene doctrine that they were the remnant, then, there now developed the doctrine that they were the *true* Israel under a new covenant. Out of it there came to the Essenes an increasing sense of their own importance. Then, as their apocalyptic ideas developed as they began to look for a Messiah of Aaron and a Messiah of Israel, they came also to think of themselves as the Elect who should be the judges of the peoples and nations at the end of days.

They also came to believe that God had ordained all things in the beginning, and that the world's history was but the working out of his decrees. Consequently, they thought the wisest man was the prophet or seer because he had the ability to discover these things. Believing as they did that the prediction of future events could be found in the writings of the prophets, they searched all ancient Scriptures, hoping to find there a guide to their own times. We have seen the practice illustrated in the Commentary on Habakkuk, Nahum, Micah and Psalm 37. As a result of these and other similar writings, the later Essenes cherished their own sacred literature as a collection of secret teachings in which "hidden things," unknown to anyone else, had been revealed to them.

Beside the commanding sense of purpose and significance achieved by the Essenes by the time of the earthquake in Judea in 31 B.C., there was one other aspect of their movement which would seem virtually to have guaranteed their continued existence, namely, the structure of the community as a social unit. The Manual of Discipline shows what an extraordinarily tight-knit structure the Essenes had created. We have it in its final and fully developed form, of course, and we know from the fragment literature from the Qumran caves that there were earlier and less complex "editions." Consequently, we cannot rely too heavily on it for the practices of the earlier period. Nevertheless, the very development of the Manual exhibited by the fragment literature and the corrections in our copy of the Manual itself is our clearest evidence that its rules existed in the Essene community for a long time previous to the writing of the edition which was found in Qumran Cave 1.

The Manual of Discipline reveals to us a movement able to sustain itself because it possessed a special structure of its own which was capable of perpetuating it. How far the disciplines of the group had been worked out in the early period we cannot say. It is clear, however, that by the time of the earthquake, enough structure had already been achieved to enable the group to hold together. Enough disciplines had already been established to assure its functioning. Its purpose and its mission were clear enough to make the enterprise seem worth while to its members. For all these reasons, bewildered and lost as they may often have felt, they carried on in part because they wanted to, in part because they did not know what else to do, but most of all because they knew how.

To sum up, at least three profound convictions held the Essene movement together during the long years at Jerusalem or wherever the members were while the Community Center at Qumran was unoccupied. First was the expectation of the end of days and all the eschatalogical beliefs that went with that concept. Both fear and hope animated them as was the case with all the millennial sects of the time. Believing that the end was near, and that it would be terrible when it came, they proposed to be ready.

Secondly, the Essenes had come to believe that they were the true Israel, the remnant of God's chosen people, and that for this reason they had a special role to play in the divine plan both at the end of days and in the interim. It was a heavy burden and a great responsibility, as well as an amazing promise for the future. According to their view, they, as God's Elect, were to be the judges of the nations when at last the day of wrath should come.

Lastly, the reverence of the Essenes for Qumran itself must surely have been an important factor in holding the movement together. As time went on and the rigors of life in the desert were forgotten, the Community House may well have taken on a special aura in the minds of the younger members, who had never known at first hand the heat and the privation of the wilderness. For them, the past would increasingly have become the golden age. Then, as yet more time passed, life at Qumran would have become translated into the dream of a utopia which they might one day bring to pass again.

Meanwhile, the day in and day out, year in and year out life of the community would have become tedious and humdrum in the extreme. The first discovery the Essenes would make at Jerusalem, once they were established there, would surprise them. Until they had actually transplanted their special way of life to a great metropolis, they would not realize the extent to which the quality of life they experienced at Qumran was due to Qumran itself. They had withdrawn from the life of Judea in order to keep clear of its evils, and to follow the Law in all purity. Back at Jerusalem they discovered that the opportunity for personal purity which Qumran provided was by no means the only value which followed upon their decision. They found that the quality of life which a group of like-minded men were able to achieve in isolation from the world, under self-imposed discipline, was the thing that had really made daily life meaningful. This they had never quite understood, even though they had lived in the midst of it.

There is no evidence in the Dead Sea Scrolls to support the thesis that long, hard years followed the removal of the Essenes to Jerusalem, as there is none even to support the thesis that it was to Jerusalem they retired. There is, however, enough evidence in the annals of men, and in the personal experience of many people, to indicate to us that it would have been so.

We are probably on pretty solid ground when we say that the Essenes had a hard time of it in their first years at Jerusalem.

during which they tried to hold to the standards and practices of Qumran in the midst of an urban center. Consequently, it would have been at Jerusalem that they discovered how much the community life at Qumran had meant to them and how dependent was the quality of life they achieved upon the Community Center itself. Doubtless some fell away. The impact of urban life upon these desert ascetics would have been very great. Others may have given up out of disillusionment or sheer tedium. But we must recall the fact that only the strictest and most religious of all the Jews would have gone out into the desert in the first place. The men who went to Qumran and stuck it out were the purists of the pure. To them the ancient ideal was of commanding importance, and their loyalty to it had been thoroughly tested. They were men who might be expected to remain loyal to the Law as they understood it even when their Community Center was destroyed and they had had to return to Jerusalem.

How they carried on at Jerusalem or elsewhere we cannot even guess. Separately perhaps, each earning his living as best he could, but meeting for a nightly communal meal, reading their own ancient books and of course forever reading and rereading the Law and the Prophets, searching out hidden meanings and discussing their thoughts earnestly with one another. Perhaps they were able to establish a community house at Jerusalem. Yet even if they did, the intrusions of the city would make their life difficult at best.

At Jerusalem the Essenes learned how to maintain sectarian existence in the midst of a great city. This is something quite different from membership in a political or religious party. There is relatively easy flow from one party to another, and the motives which lead people to join one or the other of them are various. With a sect like the Essenes, however, quite a different situation prevails. With them the strictest standards of admission were maintained. Once a person became a member, he was a member for life on pain of the severest anathemas. He was required to follow the strictest rules without deviation. Sociologically speaking, it required a high degree of adaptability on the part of the Essenes to learn to follow their old familiar ways under such radically different circumstances. That they succeeded at the task, however difficult it was, is testified to by the fact that they continued their existence as a group during this period.

11

THE RETURN

When Pompey took Jerusalem in 63 B.C., Hyrcanus II not only continued to hold the office of high priest, but he was made ethnarch as well. Antipater, the father of Herod, was his minister. A wily and able politician, Antipater became a staunch ally of Pompey and continued so until 48 B.C., when Julius Caesar defeated Pompey in Thessaly. Thereupon, Antipater became the ally of Caesar.

Julius Caesar was assassinated in 44 B.C. In the same year Antipater was also assassinated. His son Herod, who was governor of Galilee, now maneuvered to take his father's place as ruler of Palestine. Following in Antipater's dexterous footsteps, he first supported Brutus and Cassius, the fellow conspirators in the death of Caesar. When they succumbed to Mark Antony, Herod shifted his allegiance to Antony and continued to support him until Caesar Augustus became emperor of Rome in 32 B.C. Herod then transferred his support to the new emperor. Peace now reigned in both Rome and Judea. Herod held his role as king until his death in 4 B.C.

Under the firm hand of Caesar Augustus, Herod proved to be a great and efficient administrator. He was Hellenistic in spirit, but he did not force his Hellenism upon the Jews. Under him the old ideal of a religious and culturally free Israel, governed politically by a strong foreign ruler, prevailed. Israel was free once more to follow the Law.

The return of the Essenes from Jerusalem to Qumran, which took place about this time, is shrouded in as much mystery as was the exodus of forty years before. We know, however, that the return occurred sometime near or perhaps in the same year that marks the beginning of the Christian Era. A few coins found in the excavation at Khirbet Qumran date to the reign of Herod Archelaus, 4 B.C.-6 A.D. Coins of a later date are plentiful. Obviously it was about this time that the Essenes returned.

They seemed to have begun at once to repair the damage resulting from the earthquake. The debris they cleared away may still be seen close to the foundations of the building. They enlarged the buildings and lustration pools and they added new assembly halls, the largest being more than 60 feet long. The complicated water system was considerably enlarged. Two new large reservoirs were built and many smaller sumps and places for water storage were added.

Can we reconstruct in our minds the company that returned to the ruins of the Essene Community Center at the Wadi Qumran? Can we determine their motives? If we are right in assuming the difficulties in keeping the group together at Jerusalem and if we may also assume that toward the end of their sojourn there they talked more and more of the old monastery in the desert, then our picture comes into focus. The old men remembered the departed glory and the young men dreamed of recovering it. Returning to Qumran became something of an obsession for them.

The political situation doubtless was the factor, as it had been a hundred years before, that gave the final impetus to their second departure for the desert. During the early part of the Qumran period the Pharisees had been in control most of the time, but under Herod neither the Pharisees nor the Sadducees can be said to have held sway. The power of the Sanhedrin was limited by Herod's strong arm, but he left the ordering of the religious life to the people and the Jews themselves. It was a good time for Israel. Herod rebuilt the Temple, and the Law was enforced during his reign. Thus there would have been no great need to return to Qumran during his rule.

Turbulent times followed his death, however. Herod, by will, appointed his son Antipas tetrarch of Galilee and Perea. Archelaus, his elder brother, was made king of Judea, Samaria and Idumea; Philip, their half brother, was given the area north and east of the Sea of Galilee. In thus dismembering and distributing his kingdom among his sons he made the struggle for power already latent among them inevitable.

Rebellion against Archelaus at once broke out in Jerusalem. It had reached such proportions by the Passover season that he was forced to crush it with his troops. Three thousand of the rioters were killed in the conflict. Archelaus then hurried off to Rome in order to be confirmed in the office of king. In his absence, the rebellion, aggravated when a Roman officer openly robbed the Temple at Pentecost, broke out in Jerusalem again and quickly spread throughout Archelaus' entire realm. Because the rebellion had reached such proportions, the Roman governor of Syria now intervened to put it down.

Morton Scott Enslin summarizes the events that followed: "The first blow was struck in Galilee. Sepphoris, the scene of Judas' insurrection, was burned to the ground and its populace sold into slavery. Then by forced marches through Samaria— this alone of Herod's domain had refrained from insurrection— he hastened to Judea. The rebels melted before the dreaded legions. Relentlessly Varus pursued them, thoroughly dispersed, them, crucified two thousand of the ringleaders, and returned to Antioch, leaving the land numbed if not quiet. Archelaus and his brother Antipas returned to find their land in a sorry plight, many towns in ruins, the people sullen and hostile."

Caesar Augustus confirmed all three brothers in the offices Herod had bequeathed to them. During the hearings that preceded the confirmation, the debates, the claims and the counterclaims were many. We need concern ourselves with but one of these details. Among the many delegations of Jews that appeared before Augustus at this time, at least two asked that Rome annex

Palestine outright, yet another instance of the continuing desire
on the part of a small group in Israel that the nation be ruled by
one of the world's great empires, while the people were left
alone to follow the Law of the Lord as they believed they ought
to do. Again in this instance, can we not hazard the guess that
one or both of these delegations represented the Essene community, which at this time seems to have been located in
Jerusalem? In the end, the delegation that asked for annexation
succeeded. After nine years, Augustus ousted Archelaus from
office and made his territory into a Roman imperial province, to
be governed by a procurator. Pontius Pilate was the fifth person
to occupy this office.

In reconstructing the historical background of the second
exodus of the Essenes to Qumran, we cannot really discern the
kind of events that would have driven them to such a decision.
Granting the predisposition to attempt life in the wilderness
again that rose out of romantic idealization of the past, what
do we find in the political scene that would give the added
impetus so great a decision would require? Only the bloody
rebellion that took place on the death of Herod would seem
to fit the pattern. That would mean the first Essenes went back
to Qumran in 4 or perhaps 3 B.C., oddly enough at about the
same time that Jesus was born in Bethlehem. Perhaps their
appearance before Augustus, asking that their native land be made
a province of the Roman empire, the initial denial of the request,
and their exodus to Qumran are all part of a single pattern.

The reign of Archelaus is noted for its ineptitude and its
gratuitous affronts to Jewish sensibilities, but it was peaceful, and
he did not interfere with the religious practices of the people.
This state of affairs hardly explains the decision of a group of
ascetic-minded men to take up life in the Judean wilderness.
They may have done so merely as a result of internal develop-
ments in the movement that had nothing to do with external
events. The possibility can never be overlooked, and the evidence
from the coins indicates that Qumran may not have been occupied
for the second time until A.D. 6 when Judea became a Roman
province, or possibly even after that.

In any case, for whatever particular reason over and above the desire to return, the Community Center was rebuilt and enlarged within a decade or so after 4 B.C. Once more its halls were busy with the passing of many feet. Its pottery wheel turned again, its kitchens provided food, the reservoirs and catch basins were full, manuscripts began again to come from the scriptorium, and neophytes, wishing to join the order, filled the caves round about. Those who returned found life at Qumran to be more arduous than they had expected, but they also found that the fellowship was rich and rewarding. The desert, the old house, and the isolation worked anew their magic, and the Qumran Community was born again.

Meanwhile their beliefs were slowly, though steadily, changing. The change is most vividly mirrored in the Commentary on Psalm 37 of our Old Testament, which is in the fragment literature. It dates from early in the Christian Era. The few lines that have been preserved yield very interesting information. The form is similar to the Habakkuk Commentary. Bits of Scripture are interlarded with explanations of the hidden meanings to be found within them. The lines suggest the manner and mood of the writing. Our fragment begins at verse 8.

". . . *Cease from anger and forsake wrath, and be not inflamed with a fury which leads only to evil, for the wicked will be cut off.* Its interpretation concerns all those who turn back to the Law, who do not refuse to return from their wickedness, for all those who rebel against turning back from their iniquity will be cut off. *And those who are waiting for Yahweh will inherit the earth.* Its interpretation: they are the Congregation of His Elect who do His will. *And in a little while the wicked will be no more, and I shall look carefully for his place, and it will be gone.* Its interpretation concerns all the wickedness at the end of the completion of forty years when there will not be found in the earth any wicked man. *And the humble shall inherit the earth and they shall delight in the abundance of peace.* Its interpretation concerns the Congregation of the Poor who accept the Season of Affliction, and they will be delivered from all the snares. . . ."

There follows a break where a portion of the document is

missing. It begins again with the last part of a comment on verse
18 which reads, "The Lord knoweth the days of the upright:
and their inheritance shall be forever." Then the commentary
begins:

". . . the Penitents of the Desert who will live a thousand generations. . . . Man and to his seed for ever. *And in the days of
famine they will be satisfied but the wicked will perish.* Its interpretation is that He will keep them alive in famine in the
Season of Affliction . . . will perish in famine and in plague all
who did [do?] not go out . . . the Congregation of His Elect. *And
those who love Yahweh are like the preciousness of lambs* [?].
Its interpretation is that the Congregation of His Elect will be
the Chieftains and Princes . . . sheep in the midst of their pas-
tures. *All of them will be consumed like smoke.* The interpretation concerns the Princes of Wickedness who have oppressed His
holy people, who will perish like the smoke of a flame in the
wind. *The wicked man borrows and does not repay, but the
righteous person is gracious and giving. For those whom He has
blessed will inherit the earth, and those whom He has cursed
will be cut off.* Its interpretation concerns the Congregation of
the Poor . . . the inheritance of all the . . . will inherit the
Mount of the Height of Israel, and His holy people will delight
. . . *will be cut off.* They are the ruthless ones of the people, the
wicked of Israel who will be cut off and will be destroyed for
ever. *By Yahweh are Man's steps secured* and in all *his ways does
He delight; for though* he fall he will not be hurled headlong,
for Yahweh is supporting his hand. Its interpretation concerns
the priest, the Teacher of Righteousness who . . . has established
him to build for Him the Congregation of His Elect. . . . A lad
was I and now am I old and yet I have not seen a righteous man
forsaken nor his seed seeking food. All the day *he is gracious and
lends and his* seed is a blessing. . . ."

Several things are immediately apparent. The order has now
developed a set of names for itself. The members think of themselves as "the Congregation of His [God's] Elect." They are "the
Congregation of the Poor" and "the Penitents of the Desert." The
last name indicates that they were a desert group at the time

this commentary was written. The emerging of these names can be seen in the Habakkuk Commentary. There the author referred to the Essenes as "the doers of the Law," "His [God's] Elect," "the poor" and "the men of truth." But these designations are primarily descriptive phrases rather than proper names.

The same is true in the Damascus Document. The document begins: "And now listen, all of you who know righteousness and understand the works of God." If at that time there had been a proper name which the members called themselves, surely it would have been used instead of the phrase "you who know righteousness." The author also writes: "And now listen all you who have entered the covenant." This is more of a descriptive phrase than it is a name. The same is true of the phrase "elect of Israel," which is not actually a proper name as it is used here. The Manual of Discipline seems to represent an intermediate stage, for in it are such phrases as "the sons of Light," "the sons of Truth" and "the Men of Perfect Holiness."

One of the most significant insights into the later phase of the Essene movement that is to be found in the Commentary on Psalm 37 is their description of themselves as "the Congregation of His [God's] Elect." This appellation, used at least four times in the small fragment that has been preserved, has now undoubtedly become a name by which they are accustomed to think of themselves, and shows how central a place the doctrine that they are the elect of Israel has come to hold in their thinking.

We have already seen how this belief slowly emerged in Essene thought. As Israel departed further from the ancient way and as they, the remnant, clung desperately to it, they gradually developed the doctrine that they were the true keepers of the Law, the true Israel and the true Elect. This led them to believe that Israel, having broken the covenant, forfeited her old position. Thus the Essenes thought of themselves as the Elect of God under the new covenant. The apocalyptic note, always present in their thinking, now became more dominant. They still expected that the end of days would soon come. When it came, the Congregation of His Elect would inherit the earth. After the completion of forty years, "The wicked will be cut off" and "there will not be found in the earth any wicked man." "The Penitents of the Desert will live a thousand generations. . . . The Congregation of His Elect will be the Chieftains and Princes. . . . The Congregation of the Poor will inherit the Mount of Height."

Apocalyptic elements are also evident in the Habakkuk Commentary and in the Manual of Discipline. In the Manual the doctrine of the new covenant is clearly set forth. The new member is said to "enter the covenant." The entire community renews the covenant annually. The premise upon which the Habakkuk Commentary was written appears to be that the end is imminent and "into the hand of his Elect God will deliver the judgment of all the nations and by their chastisement, all the wicked among his people will be punished." In the Commentary on Psalm 37 this has become much more explicit.

Lastly, in the Psalm Commentary the Teacher of Righteousness is given a much more exalted role than in the earlier documents. Now God is thought to have "established him to build for Him the Congregation of His Elect." This role is not one which the Teacher of Righteousness took upon himself; it is one into which God cast him in order to fulfill his own particular purposes. The Essenes were strict determinists, who believed that God knew all things and foreordained them. The Essenes believed that God's purpose was to establish the Teacher of Righteousness in order that he might build the Congregation of the Elect. There is here no suggestion of the Messiah, nor that the Teacher of Righteousness was a prophet. It is obvious, however, that by this time the Essenes considered the Teacher of Righteousness as a special emissary, commissioned by Yahweh to do a special task among his people Israel.

Nevertheless, the Essenes continued to resemble the Pharisees in many ways, although the two groups had long been separated. Both insisted upon the necessity for strict observance of the Law of Moses. The Manual of Discipline reads: "Everyone who comes into the council of the community shall enter into the covenant of God. He shall take it upon himself by a binding oath to turn to the Law of Moses, according to all that he commanded." The teaching of the Pharisees was similar. Probably the only difference between them lay in the fact that the Essenes, as the stricter group, would have tended to change less, so their teaching would have tended to be more archaic. The Pharisees, on the other hand, were the group in Israel who, attempting to keep the Law, elaborated rules to interpret the Scripture so that the righteous man might know what to do.

The resemblance between the Pharisees and the Essenes was such that their differences have been said to be no greater than the differences between the various groups of Pharisees into which the Pharisees were divided in the time of Jesus. They were organized into societies called haburoth and the members were called haburim. Both required candidates for admission to observe strict rules of ritualistic purity and both required a period of probation before admission.

Doubtless the two groups influenced each other throughout their existence. Doubtless also there was some recruiting of members by each from the other. Those Pharisees who wanted a more strict observance of the Law would have gone to Qumran and those Essenes who thought the practices of their sect too extreme, or who found life in the desert too arduous, might well have returned to the cities of Judah or Galilee to follow the more tolerant and less exacting way of the Pharisees.

The essential difference between the two is the Essene belief that now they are the Elect of God, who, living under a new covenant, will be the judges of the nations at the end of days. No such view was entertained by the Pharisees. They, with the rest of Jewry, believed that Israel was still God's chosen people, his elect among the nations, and that the old covenant was still valid. Their emphasis on the Law was built upon this premise. The Essene emphasis on the Law was built upon the premise that they themselves were the Elect.

There are few who dispute the evolution and development of the religion of Israel. The concept of what the true religion consisted in surely changed in spite of all the efforts of the prophets, and latterly the Essenes to hold to the old way. But that is not what is important. Israel's genius did not consist in freezing her religion at any given point; but rather in the recurring demand that the children of Israel remain loyal to the covenant between Yahweh and his people and that they not permit their loyalty to be watered down by compromises with the religions of their neighbors.

Upon this the Hasidim insisted; for this the Maccabees fought; for this the Pharisees divided with John Hyrcanus; for this the Essenes separated from the Pharisees; and for this the Teacher of Righteousness challenged the Wicked Priest. In the first century B.C., loyalty to the Law was the ideal of both the Essenes and the Pharisees, but by the first century A.D. the Essenes had added a new twist to the doctrine that was all their own. They had given up trying to hold all Israel to the ancient ideal, and had come to think of themselves as the bearers of the covenant that Israel had abandoned. As Israel had dared to think of herself as unique among the nations, so the Essenes now dared to think of themselves as unique among the Israelites. In their sense of uniqueness, their belief in a unique leader, the Teacher of Righteousness, held a conspicuous place. These were ideas fraught with possibility. How rich a fruit they bore we shall now see.

12

JOHN THE BAPTIST

John the Baptist stood squarely in the tradition of the prophets of Israel. Like his noble forebears, he challenged the priesthood of the Temple and denounced the secular ruler of the state. Like them he called the people of his nation back to a better way and demanded that they live according to the teachings of their own religious tradition. His contemporaries did not hesitate to compare him to Elijah, whom they considered to have been the greatest of the prophets. Jesus himself said there was none among those born of woman greater than John.

His preaching was in the prophetic tradition. "You brood of vipers," he cried, "who warned you to flee from the wrath to come? Bear fruits that befit repentance, and do not begin to say to yourselves, 'We have Abraham as our father.'" The children of Israel had heard words like these many times before. For centuries their prophets had denounced them for their sins, and they were accustomed to it. They had often been told that mere birth into the community of Israel was not enough. Descent from Abraham would not save them; only fruits that befitted repentance could do that. "Every tree that does not bear good fruit is cut down and thrown into the fire," said John.

Such was the punishment the people should receive unless they mended their ways.

When the people asked John what they must do to show the fruits of repentance, he was explicit: "He who has two coats, let him share with him who has none. He who has food let him do likewise." To the tax collectors, he said, "Collect no more than is appointed you." To the soldiers, he said, "Rob no one by violence or by false accusation, and be content with your wages." His too was the ancient demand of the prophet Amos for righteousness. His call for mercy and loving-kindness was like that of Hosea, Micah and Jeremiah.

When John the Baptist denounced Herod's marrying Herodias, he allied himself irrevocably with Israel's greatest prophets. Long before, Nathan criticized David for coveting Bathsheba and Elijah inveighed against Ahab and Jezebel. The popular story of John and Herodias and Salome as presented in imaginative literature has obscured both the real reason for John's death and the true stature of the man. He was executed for sedition and for the criticizing of Herod.

There was, however, an important difference between John the Baptist and the prophets. They were often persecuted and driven from the community, but we have no record of the execution of any of the early prophets of Israel. The prophets were looked upon as divine emissaries and, even under the most trying of circumstances, they were heard. But times changed. John the Baptist dealt, not with a descendant of the house of David, but with Herod the Idumean, who was no true son of Israel and who enjoyed such powers as he had at the sufferance of Rome.

If John the Baptist had a precursor in Israel, he was the Teacher of Righteousness whose boldness in denouncing an earlier ruler may also have cost him his life. We know more regarding the activities of the Baptist than of the Teacher of Righteousness, but, insofar as we can reconstruct their stories, the parallels between the two are remarkable. Both denounced the ruler of the state for departing from the Law of the Lord and both seem to have been equally vehement in denouncing the people for their laxity. Both apparently felt that withdrawal from an apostate Israel was the best course to follow and both lived apart in the desert.

There are, however, more impressive reasons for connecting John the Baptist with the Essene sect than the similarities between his pattern of life and that of the Teacher of Righteousness. Many of these were noted long before the discovery of the Dead Sea Scrolls. It had long since been observed, for example, that Pliny's reference to the Essene colony placed it in the very region in the Judean desert in which the New Testament said John lived. Some scholars had also noted that the ascetic practices of John, as recorded in the New Testament, were remarkably similar to those of the Essenes, as reported by Philo and Josephus. In fact, the question of the relationship between John the Baptist and the Essenes had been actively considered for at least a hundred and fifty years. An extensive literature had featured the subject. Jesus himself was often likened to the Essenes.

F. C. Conybeare, a distinguished scholar of fifty years ago, wrote in Hastings' *Dictionary of the Bible*: "Some writers, impressed with the fact that Jesus constantly inveighed against the Pharisees and Sadducees, but never against the members of the third of the great Jewish sects, who yet must have everywhere confronted him, have inferred that he and John the Baptist, his precursor, were Essenes. The silence of the Gospels about the Essenes is certainly remarkable; and there are many striking traits in common between the Essenes and the earliest Christians." He listed nine traits and gave illustrations of each.

The linking of John the Baptist to the Essenes is further strengthened by the remarkable conjunction of both time and place. John dwelt in the same desert, a wilderness east of Jerusalem and north and west of the Dead Sea, into which the Essenes withdrew to build their Community Center. During the time that John was preaching in this region, the Essene community was a flourishing enterprise. The archeological evidence from Qumran makes this quite clear. John the Baptist could not have been ignorant of the community, nor could the Essenes have been uninformed about him. Their proximity makes the presumption of some kind of connection almost inevitable.

When their messages are considered together the similarity is even more remarkable. For example, all four Gospels agree that John in the desert was fulfilling the prophecy of Isaiah, "The voice of one crying in the wilderness, prepare ye the way of the Lord. Make his paths straight." In relatively few instances do all four Gospels so exactly agree upon a point. According to the Manual of Discipline, the Essenes used the same quotation to describe their purpose in going to the desert: "When these things come to pass for the community in Israel, by these regulations they shall be separated from the midst of the session of the men of error to go to the wilderness to prepare there the way of the Lord; as it is written, 'In the wilderness prepare the way of the Lord; make straight in the desert a highway for our God.' This is the study of the law, as he commanded through Moses, to do according to all that has been revealed from time to time, and as the prophets revealed by his Holy Spirit."

The idea of a Day of Yahweh and of the coming of a Branch of the house of David were already old in Israel in the time of John the Baptist. Since the days of Amos, Israel had heard about a day of wrath, known as the "Day of Yahweh." Isaiah, Jeremiah, Zephaniah, Zechariah, Joel and Malachi had all prophecied its coming. The idea that a "branch of the root of Jesse," a descendant of David, would one day sit on Israel's ancient throne again, was likewise of ancient origin. There was nothing messianic in this realistic and nationalistic concept, which represented little more than national selfconsciousness and the desire for national independence. The prophets spoke of an earthly kingdom, but gradually a supernatural quality entered and in time it was interpreted to mean that a new king, through the intervention of Yahweh, would be seated on the throne.

The idea of the branch appeared first in the seventh century B.C. The Deuteronomist, on behalf of Yahweh, wrote, "I will raise up a prophet to speak in my name." During the period of her exile, Israel began to fasten her hopes upon this promise. Isaiah had spoken of the coming of an offshoot of Jesse, a "branch growing out of his roots." This became identified in the Hebrew mind with Deuteronomy's promise of a "prophet." Jeremiah said that the Lord would "raise up unto David a righteous branch, and that he shall reign as king." Zechariah wrote: "I will bring forth my servant the branch, and will remove the mighty of the land in that day."

Meanwhile, however, a third idea, absorbed from the Iranian philosophy of Persia, entered Jewish thought. This was the belief in a final catastrophe in which the world would be destroyed and a new world, purged of sin, would take its place. Such an idea would be, of course, neither novel nor uncongenial to the pious Jew. He knew that Yahweh, the God of Israel, had once before nearly destroyed the earth by a great flood.

The Iranian concept was more vivid and more precise than this, however. Carl Kraeling has written: "In Persian eschatology, the mountains which are made of metal melt at the end of the world and the molten metal pours over the earth like a river. All men pass into this river of molten metal and in so doing are either purified or destroyed. Since in Persian thought this conception, already presupposed in the Gathas, is part of a well coordinated system of eschatology, it is entirely possible that we have here the ultimate source of all these realistic interpretations of the function of fire in the final judgment, and thus also the source of Daniel's river of fire."

The Book of Daniel shows how Persian eschatological ideas were absorbed by the Israelites during the second century B.C. The Day of Yahweh is present, although the idea of the branch of the house of David is not yet associated with it. Neither the "branch" nor its later development, the concept of the Messiah, appears in Daniel, which speaks only of "The Ancient of Days" and "One like unto a Son of Man," which, for the author, was a poetic paraphrase for Israel.

Persian eschatology cemented the Israelitic ideas of the branch and the Day of Yahweh. This is seen in the Book of Enoch, written in the first century B.C., where the separate elements are brought together for the first time. The "son of man" is no longer Israel; he is the branch of the house of Jesse. He is the agent who will usher in the day of wrath and he is the judge between the righteous and the wicked. He is the supernatural agent by whom the new supernatural kingdom of Israel will make its appearance.

The popular concept of the Messiah does not appear in the Old Testament, although, of course, the word for "Messiah," which means "anointed," is often used. Because he was king, David is spoken of as "the Lord's anointed"; Saul and Samuel are referred to in the same terms. Being anointed was a status held by kings, high priests and patriarchs.

When the idea of the Messiah as we understand the term was taking form, "the Lord's anointed" was not considered as a supernatural agent who would usher in the new age. The identification of the "anointed" with the "branch" and the "son of man" came later. The author of the book of Enoch first drew these concepts together and applied them to the same personage. It follows that the habit of speaking of the one who would usher in the last days and who would judge the people as the "Messiah" or "the Lord's anointed" did not make its appearance until the first century B.C. That is why the term "the Lord's anointed" used in this special sense nowhere appears in the Old Testament.

The idea was still new in the time of John the Baptist. It never became strong in official Judaism and attained little currency until after the destruction of Jerusalem in A.D. 70. In fact, down to the discovery of the Dead Sea Scrolls, many scholars felt that in spite of the references in Enoch, the fully developed messianic idea did not appear at all until after the beginning of the Christian Era.

It is risky to try to be too exact about dates, but it would appear that the fully developed idea of the Messiah was arrived at by the Essenes at least as early as the time when the book of Enoch was written. That would be at least fifty years before John the Baptist preached about it at the River Jordan. The Manual of Discipline reads: "There shall come a prophet and the Messiahs of Aaron and Israel." Members of the community are to obey the rules until that happy event takes place. The Damascus Document speaks of those who follow the way of the Essenes "until a Messiah shall arise from Aaron and from Israel."

A yet more striking parallel between the Essenes and John the Baptist is to be found in the rite of baptism. There were three stages in the baptism of John: repentance of past misdeeds, immersion and forgiveness. The same steps seem to have been practiced among the Essenes. They laid great stress on repentance. They refer to themselves as the "Penitents of the Desert" in the Commentary on Psalm 37. The Damascus Document calls their covenant the "Covenant of Repentance." It requires the members to "confess before God, saying, 'Indeed we have acted wickedly, both we and our fathers by walking contrarywise against the ordinances of the covenant.'" According to the Manual of Discipline, a state of repentance is prerequisite to baptism: "They shall not enter the water in order to be permitted to touch the sacred food of the holy men, for they will not be cleansed unless they have turned from their evil."

The remission of sins, central in the preaching of John the Baptist, is also a part of the Essene concept. The Manual of Discipline says of the individual who enters the covenant, "All his iniquities will be atoned . . . he will be cleansed of all his iniquities." We cannot rely too completely on language here, particularly in regard to details, because the exact meaning of the Hebrew is not always clear. The translations of these passages may vary considerably. The evidence is ample enough, however, to enable us to distinguish a parallel with the practices of John the Baptist.

The Manual of Discipline and the Damascus Document nowhere explicitly prescribe immersion. This fact has led some to wonder whether baptism held the place in the Essene movement that is usually supposed. But the difficulty is more imaginary than real. Neither of these documents appears to be a complete set of directions. Apparently the Essenes wrote down only those regulations they thought ought to be recorded. It is said that the first law codes, like that of Hammurabi and those that preceded it, contained only new laws, for everyone knew the old laws.

The best evidence of the practice of ritual washings and of baptism among the Essenes has been offered by the archeologists rather than by the students of the Scroll literature. Many basins, having the obvious purpose of ritual washings, were found at Khirbet Qumran. Large pools, entered by broad steps, suggest such a use. The Manual of Discipline speaks of sprinkling, and this, rather than immersion, may have been the Essene practice. Certainly in an area where water was as precious as it was at Qumran, sprinkling would seem to be a more logical rite.

There are parallels elsewhere in Judaism to the practice of baptism. The baptism of converts to Judaism prevailed in the synagogues at the time. We know that the synagogue was by no means lacking in spiritual emphasis, for the Jews were devout as a people. The practice of confession coupled with the concept of the remission of sins was familiar to them.

The practice of baptism among the Essenes and in Judaism had a common ancestry. There was, however, a difference between the two. In the synagogue, the baptism of proselytes was thought to wash away the defilement of the convert who, as a non-Jew, had not observed the Law. Baptism for the Essenes was intended to cleanse the Jews themselves. No baptism of Jews was considered necessary in the synagogue.

Was there a difference between Essene baptism and the rite as practiced by John the Baptist? The answer to this question admits of no debate, for the difference between the two was marked. Essene baptism was an internal affair for those initiates who were "entering the covenant." Possibly it was repeated during their ceremony of "renewing the covenant." If so, it was still limited to the Essene community itself. Their rite was by Essenes and for Essenes only. John the Baptist, on the contrary, took his baptism to the world.

William H. Brownlee suggests that his missionary zeal distinguishes him from the Essenes, that he outspiritualized Israel and the Essenes as well. John may well have been one of the boys the Essenes are said to have adopted, a practice Josephus mentions. "They neglect wedlock," he writes, "but choose out other persons' children, while they are pliable, and fit for learning, and esteem them to be of their kindred, and form them according to their own manners." When John reached maturity, thinks Brownlee, he carried the Essene teaching one step further. He extended the need of repentance as taught by the Essenes to all Israel. They accepted those whom they deemed upon their confession and repentence to be worthy. All others they seem to have relegated to the congregation of Belial. Charles T. Fritsch concurs in this judgment.

John the Baptist became a missionary and perhaps tried to make the Essenes into a missionary movement. In this he reversed the Essene concept, which originally had been developed by men who felt they had no other course but to withdraw into the wilderness and prepare there the way of the Lord. John, who thought of himself as the voice crying in that wilderness, did his best to prepare the way of the Lord for all Israel. He believed with Isaiah that the wilderness was the place to do it; but he felt that not only the novices, camped around Qumran, and the members of the more exclusive inner circle, but all the descendants of Aaron and Israel should be called to repentance and, upon confession, should be baptized unto the remission of sin.

Such a supposition provides reasonable answers for many of our questions. If the Essene movement tended toward rigidity, toward making more regulations and applying them more strictly, then they must slowly, but no less surely, have lost sight of their original ideal. With the multiplication of rules, life tends to become centered upon them and less attention inevitably is given to doing the things the rules are supposed to advance. The Manual of Discipline seems to indicate that the spiritual emphasis was always central with the Essenes—yet the very detailed prescriptions of the Manual, and perhaps of other documents, must surely have led the community toward emphasizing the letter more than the spirit of their many regulations. This state of affairs would then have become apparent to some of the members who had come to Qumran because of the genuinely spiritual quality of the community. If the Essenes were mere rule followers, how these men would have thought, were they better than the legalistic Pharisees? Such a question would have caused at least a part of the Essenes to insist that the spiritual emphasis in the Manual of Discipline was essential. All were guilty and repentance was necessary. This message ought now to be carried to all Israel.

Does the foregoing suggestion provide us with a sufficient

explanation of John the Baptist's breaking with the Essenes and taking their teachings to all Israel? It cannot be shown that he was required to leave the movement in order to maintain his high spiritual ideals. Furthermore, to break with the Essenes was a step not to be taken lightly. We know of the curses which the Essenes heaped upon the backslider. Perhaps the central motive in John the Baptist's becoming an apostate Essene was a conviction that the Essene teaching ought no longer to be kept secret. As we have seen, the Essenes believed that they could follow the Law in a superior way because hidden meanings in it had been revealed to them and to them alone. The Manual of Discipline speaks of those outside the covenant as not knowing "the hidden things in which they have gone astray." Why then was John now ready to reveal these secrets to the multitude and to break his pledge to the Essenes in doing so?

We find the answer in the belief both of the Essenes and of John that the kingdom was at hand and the Messiah was soon to come. Both expected the end of days and the coming of the Messiah. The Essenes prepared themselves for the day of wrath, confident that, as God's Elect, they would be the judges of the nations when the time came. But John apparently thought all Israel should be warned of their impending doom and urged to repent and be saved. So he left the Essene colony and at Bethany beyond Jordan and at Aenon near Salim he began his preaching to the multitudes and his baptizing of the repentant. Both these towns were trading posts on important highways near the River Jordan. They were places where a preacher would find crowds to listen to him, especially at festival time. And the crowds he wanted came to him from all over Judea.

His call to repent would not account for the crowds which apparently went into the desert to hear this strange prophet speak; nor would his appeal be found in his announcement that the end of days is at hand. Doubtless he was a man of great personal power, but surely he had a novel message that also seemed important. If John were now making public what had been a more or less secret teaching of the Essenes, we may readily understand his popularity, especially if we add to that the awesome reminder that the kingdom was at hand. The people had previously heard of their need to repent, of the possibility of the end of days, and perhaps of the anointed of the Lord. But none before had combined these emphases. This, out of the Essene teaching, John did for them. The people heard him gladly, and they were baptized because what we said made sense.

Except for the story of the tragic end of the Essene colony at Qumran as told by the archeologists, our knowledge of their movement is concluded with the little we know about John the Baptist. We can only guess at what happened when the Community Center was destroyed.

Whether the Essenes then dispersed, or whether they were slaughtered or sold into slavery by the Romans, we do not know. In any case the end was tragic. Archeological evidence makes clear that the Community Center was destroyed by the Romans. After A.D. 70, it was used as a Roman outpost. The halls were broken up into smaller rooms. It was occupied briefly during the second Jewish revolt A.D. 132-135, and there were brief and unimportant Arab occupations. The Essenes never returned to take their precious manuscripts from the caves. Their scrolls remained there until a series of fortunate accidents were to place a few of them in our hands nineteen centuries later.

13

SIMILARITIES BETWEEN JESUS AND THE ESSENES

If in relating John the Baptist to the Dead Sea Scrolls we enter an area where dispassionate discussion begins to be difficult, we move into a much more electric atmosphere when we consider the Scrolls in relation to Jesus Christ. His life on earth is in some sense history because he lived as a historical person in historical times. He is also an object of faith for millions of people, and this tends at times to obscure the historical material relating to his life. Yet if we are to discover what, if any, relationship exists between the Dead Sea Scrolls and Jesus called Christ, we must examine the evidence.

The greatest difficulty we face in comparing Jesus of Nazareth and the Essene sect is that we really know so little about each of them. We have seen the limits of our information about the Essenes. Our knowledge of Jesus is confined to the four Gospels and what snatches of information we have been able to discover in the Epistles of Paul and the Acts of the Apostles. Our problem is complicated by the fact that scholars have long since recognized that the evidence of the Gospels is sometimes contradictory. Yet they are the primary source of information; in fact they are virtually the only source.

We need to remember some of the things which scholars during the past century and a half have learned about the Gospels. The most obvious is that the Gospels do not always agree. We have also learned that back of the Gospels are oral traditions, and that these, too, show a variance. The Gospels were written in different times and places by different men and for different purposes. The earliest, the Gospel of Mark, was written at least a generation after Jesus passed from the human scene. The others were written perhaps two or more generations after the crucifixion. We know, through detailed studies of the Gospels, that the Jewish habit of compiling and editing ancient manuscripts prevailed among the early Christians. Generations of scholarship have even enabled the scholars to suppose the existence of a manuscript, now lost, which Matthew and Luke used. The problem for the historian is to get behind the manuscripts to the oral traditions and thence to the events from which they took their rise.

An obstacle in our study of Jesus Christ from the historical point of view is that even such sources as we possess are not themselves history, but rather polemics, sermons or exhortations which were never intended to be used primarily as records of facts. Each of the Gospels was written for a particular purpose, and we must keep those purposes in mind if we are to achieve an objectivity that the authors never possessed nor intended.

The many similarities between the teachings of Jesus and the teachings of the Essenes, as recorded in our sources, fall into two groups: those that Jesus, the Essenes and Judaism have in common; and those that only Jesus and the Essenes have in common, similarities not found elsewhere in Judaism. The similarities found in Jesus, the Essenes and the rest of Judaism show, of course, that as Jews they had the same cultural heritage and, consequently, thought alike in many ways. The Essenes and Jesus, like all good Jews, believed, for instance, in Yahweh, the God of Israel, and they believed that Moses received the Law at Yahweh's hands and gave it to the people when he had descended Mount Sinai.

Jesus began his public ministry by preaching "The kingdom of God is at hand. Repent and believe that this good news which

I bring to you is true." Repentance was a central emphasis for the Essenes and also for John the Baptist. It was an element in the teaching of the Pharisees, too, but for them the doctrine had not the eschatological implications it had for Jesus and John the Baptist.

Such a similarity between Jesus and the Essenes assumes importance for three reasons. First, such teachings are central for both. Second, while they are found elsewhere in Israel, they are by no means found everywhere. Third, each of these conjunctions, when added to others, becomes a significant element in a total cumulative pattern of similarity.

Another similarity between Jesus and the Essenes, found elsewhere in Judaism, is in the place of the communal meal. In the life of the Essene community, it acquired nearly a sacramental quality. The same thing is seen in the account of the Last Supper of Jesus and the disciples, as reported in all four Gospels. The central elements in the two ceremonies are the same: eating together in fellowship with chosen companions, the ritualistic blessing and the serving of bread and wine. This practice was common in Israel at the time, but a peculiar importance was given to it by both Jesus and the Essenes.

A striking similarity may, furthermore, be observed between the Essenes and Jesus in their stating of the principle and the practice of brotherhood. Both, of course, derived the principle from Judaism where it was formulated by the Deuteronomists at least as early as the seventh century B.C. It has been closely associated with the teaching of Jesus and its practice is reflected in the idyllic picture that shines through the Gospels of the intimate sense of fellowship that existed between Jesus and his disciples, and also in his compassion toward people generally.

That a sense of fellowship pervaded the Qumran community is not only clear from Philo and Josephus, but we have no difficulty illustrating it from the Manual of Discipline. There we read that the members are each to "reprove his neighbor in truth and humility, and loyal love for each one." They are to let their deeds "shine in the heart of man, and to make straight before him all the ways of true righteousness . . . to induce a spirit of humility, and slowness to anger, and great compassion, and eternal goodness . . . abundance of steadfast love for all the sons of truth." The members are called upon "to practice truth, unity and humility, righteousness and justice and loyal love, and to walk humbly in all their ways."

Both the Essenes and Jesus believed deeply and implicitly in the Law of Moses as Israel's directive for conduct. Jesus said, "Think not that I am come to destroy the law or the phophets. I am not come to destroy but to fulfill. For verily I say unto you, till heaven and earth pass away, one jot or tittle shall in no way pass away from the law." Furthermore, both the Essenes and Jesus looked for the coming of the Lord's anointed, and both looked for the end of days to come soon.

Both the Essenes and Jesus held the Scripture in the highest regard. Both believed that gaining a knowledge of God's will through the study of the Scriptures was of paramount importance. "What did Moses command you?" asked Jesus, when questioned about divorce. "Have you not read this scripture?" he inquired on another occasion. And to the Sadducees he said, "Ye know neither the scripture nor the power of God." Evidence of the Essenes' reverence for the Scriptures is manifest from the Qumran caves.

Both Jesus and the Essenes believed that conflict is inevitable. The War Scroll, the Psalms and the doctrine of the two spirits in man in the Manual of Discipline give ample evidence of the Essene thought. The idea of conflict, though not ordinarily associated with Jesus, is surely to be discerned in such words as: "Think not that I came to send peace on earth: I came not to send peace, but a sword. . . . I came to set a man against his father and a daughter against her mother. A man's foes shall be they of his own household."

More parallels like these are, of course, a result of their common background in Judaism. Like the Pharisees, both believed in the eternal life with its rewards and punishments, and both believed in a final judgment at the end of days, a concept less prominent elsewhere. Both laid great emphasis on the spiritual, the supreme quality we find in Jesus.

Jesus demanded from his disciples an unswerving singleness
of purpose, the kind of total loyalty that characterizes the Essenes. They demanded that those who joined their order should
give up worldly goods and break human ties. The severity of the
words of Jesus in exacting loyalty from his followers is, if anything, even greater. We sometimes forget how uncompromising
Jesus' demands were. For example, he said that no man can serve
two masters, God and mammon. But he also said, "He that loveth
father or mother more than me is not worthy of me," and on
another occasion, "Follow me" and "Leave the dead to bury their
own dead," and yet again, "No one who puts his hand to the
plow, and looks back is fit for the kingdom of God."

Fortitude, we know, was an outstanding characteristic of the
Essenes. Jesus, too, held courage and steadfastness of purpose
in very high regard. He eloquently spoke of enduring persecution: "Blessed are those who are persecuted for righteousness'
sake, for theirs is the kingdom of heaven. Blessed are you when
men revile you and persecute you and utter all kinds of evil
against you falsely on my account. Rejoice and be glad, for your
reward is great in heaven, for so men persecuted the prophets
who were before you."

Were not these qualities found elsewhere in Israel? Most certainly. We know of the fanatical courage with which the Jews
fought from Maccabean times on and of their fierce loyalty to
the ancient religion of their people. Their determination, sacrifice
and unswerving allegiance are quite as striking as that of the
Essenes and of Jesus. The similarity shows the difficulty of com-
parisons. The value of a particular resemblance between Jesus
and the Essenes must be cumulative. No individual instance
proves anything in and of itself.

A clearer contrast, perhaps, is the weeping of Jesus over Jerusalem and the lamentation of the Essenes because she slays the
prophets. We find no such attitude among the Pharisees. That
Jesus often went out into the desert to pray may, furthermore,
suggest an affinity to the Essenes who made their home in the
desert. "Come ye apart into a desert place and rest a while,"
Jesus was accustomed to say to the disciples. The Gospel of Mark

reports that when pressed by the crowds that followed him everywhere and gave him no peace, "in the morning, a great while before day, he rose and went out to a desert place and there prayed." And it was into the same desert in which the Essenes dwelt that he spent the forty days following his baptism.

An obvious similarity between Jesus and the Essenes, not duplicated except among similar ancient ascetic groups, is the high value that both place on poverty, on meekness, and on the eschewing of worldly goods. The Manual of Discipline clearly details the ascetic ideal of the Essenes. In the Sermon on the Mount Jesus proclaimed the same doctrine by making a sharp distinction between the things of this world and spiritual values. He said, "Lay not up for yourselves treasures upon earth . . . but lay up for yourselves treasures in heaven." And again, "Be not anxious for your life, what ye shall eat, what ye shall drink, nor yet for your body what ye shall put on."

Jesus' attitude toward riches is similar to the condemnation of them characteristic of the Essenes. "Woe to you that are rich," he says in the Gospel of Luke, and in Mark he speaks of the "deceitfulness of riches," saying to the rich young ruler, "Go sell all thou hast and give it to the poor." Jesus commended poverty and meekness just as the Essenes did. "Blessed are the poor in spirit. . . . Blessed are the meek," he said. These qualities are not emphasized among the Pharisees, nor elsewhere in Judaism, except among the Therapeutae in Egypt who may have had some relationship to the Essenes.

Another parallel between Jesus and the Essenes, not otherwise found in Israel, is in their doctrine of election. By the time of Jesus, the Essenes had surely begun to look upon themselves as the Elect, bound together under a new covenant with Yahweh. This is clear from their use of the title the "Congregation of God's Elect," found in the Commentary on Psalm 37. Jesus, in the Gospel accounts, did not speak of "the elect" in the traditional Israelitic sense. For him also the concept had a special meaning. On one occasion he asked, "And will not God vindicate his elect who cry to him day and night? Will he delay long over them? I tell you he will vindicate them speedily." The implication is that the elect are not all Israel, as in Old Testament thought. The elect are a special group within Israel.

In a passage in Mark, repeated in Matthew, but omitted in Luke, Jesus, speaking of the last days, says "False Christs and false prophets will arise and show signs and wonders to lead astray, if possible, the elect." Again the elect seem to constitute a special group, not all Israel. The words from the Sermon on the Mount, "Ye are the salt of the earth" and "Ye are the light of the world," appear to mean the same thing.

The words for "the elect" and "to choose," found frequently in Matthew, Mark and Luke, are always used to indicate a small group within Israel and not Israel as a whole as in the Old Testament. "For the sake of the elect, whom he chose, [God] shortened the days [of tribulation]," Mark reports Jesus as saying. And again, "He will send out the angels and gather his elect from the four winds, from the ends of the earth to the ends of heaven." The thought in the last sentence has much wider scope than the tight little comunity at Qumran. Here "elect" could mean Israel, but the word is repeated twice in this passage and in the context plainly means a separate group in Israel.

Another similarity, not found elsewhere, is the belief in a secret knowledge. The difference between the view of Jesus and the Essenes and the views of the rest of Israel may not at first be apparent. As we know, all Israel at that time believed there were hidden meanings in the Scripture and all Israel sought to discover these meanings. The Essenes, however, believed they possessed, through the revelation of the Teacher of Righteousness and perhaps through other members of the sect, a special knowledge of these hidden meanings. Jesus, too, appears to have believed that he and the disciples possessed a special understanding of the meaning of Scripture.

For example, when Jesus was teaching in the synagogue at Nazareth, the people in astonishment asked, "Where did this man get all this? What is the wisdom given to him?" Jesus also said to the disciples, "There is nothing hid except to be made manifest; nor is anything secret except to come to light." This is close to the Essene concept that a secret teaching exists which is to be disclosed. Jesus, like John, however, apparently felt that these teachings were not to be kept within a small circle, but proclaimed to all.

Luke and Matthew report Jesus as saying, "I thank thee O Father that thou didst hide these things from the wise and understanding, and didst reveal them unto babes." But usually Jesus' utterances were even clearer. "To you it has been given to know the secrets of the kingdom of heaven," he told his disciples, "but to them it has not been given." Again he said, "This is why I speak to them in parables that seeing they may not see and hearing they may not hear; nor understand. . . . But blessed are your eyes for they see, and your ears for they hear. Truly I say to you many prophets and righteous men longed to see what you see and did not see it, and to hear what you hear, and did not hear it."

The parallel that has caused the most controversy ever since A. Dupont-Sommer first pointed it out is, of course, the parallel between Jesus and the Teacher of Righteousness. The suggestion has been widely discussed, and unfortunately much of the discussion has been so heated as to obscure the real issue. Questions such as this are asked: "Does the Teacher of Righteousness prefigure Christ?" "Does the Teacher of Righteousness destroy the uniqueness of Christ?" But the "uniqueness of Christ" is not the issue here. It is simply this: "Is there a parallel between what we know of Jesus and what we know of the Teacher of Righteousness?" The answer to that question is "yes."

The Teacher of Righteousness, a leader among his people, noted for the teaching of righteousness, either went up to Jerusalem to denounce the Wicked Priest or quite possibly he had at the time never been to Qumran. We cannot be sure whether or not he paid for his boldness with his life. Jesus of Nazareth, a leader among his people, also noted for the teaching of righteousness, went up to Jerusalem, for exactly what purpose we cannot be sure, perhaps to lay claim to Messiahship. In any case, while there he, like the Teacher of Righteousness, denounced the priests, the scribes, the Pharisees, and the Temple practices of the time. We know all too well that he paid for his boldness with his life and the manner in which he did it. There the exact parallel ends, at least as far as our knowledge is concerned. Jesus' followers soon came to look upon him as the Messiah so long expected among the people of Israel. The Essenes never thought of the Teacher of Righteousness in those terms, but, as we have seen, he came to occupy a very exalted place in their memory, and the reverence in which they held him increased as the years went on.

It would seem to be possible on the basis of the foregoing parallels to make out a remarkably good case for believing that Jesus, like John the Baptist, was raised as an Essene; and that like John he left the order on gaining his maturity and took their teachings to the common people of Galilee who heard his message gladly. It would be a very congenial theory for a great many people because it would explain many things, among them the long silence in the story of Jesus between the time when he went with his parents to the Temple at Jerusalem at age twelve, and the time when at age twenty-seven or thereabouts he came preaching into Galilee. This theory was in fact arrived at long before the Dead Sea Scrolls were ever heard of. But things are not often so easily explained especially when they are important. From the similarities between Jesus and the Essenes we are compelled to move on to the differences. For there are differences, and they are yet more striking than the similarities.

14

DIFFERENCES BETWEEN JESUS AND

THE ESSENES

If the similarities between Jesus and the Essenes are striking, the differences are more so. They loom particularly large because the number of similarities between the two creates the presumption of a connection. To cite one of the less important differences, Jesus opposed the use of oaths, but the Essenes required them. Jesus said, "You have heard that it was said to the men of old 'You shall not swear falsely,' but shall perform to the Lord what you have sworn. But I say to you, do not swear at all." After listing a number of objects by which men are accustomed to swear, he concluded, "Let what you say be simply yes or no."

According to the Manual of Discipline, an oath must be taken by "everyone who comes into the council of the community." He shall, says the Manual, "enter into the covenant of God in the sight of all who have offered themselves; and he shall take [the covenant] upon himself by a binding oath to turn to the law of Moses according to all that he commanded." The same requirement is found in the Damascus Document. Jesus' condemnation is absolute, and the Essene requirement is final. In fact, Jesus seems almost to have been thinking of the requirements in the Damascus Document where the importance of fulfilling one's oath is set forth at some length.

It may seem that we do not prove much by so small a contrast. Yet a small difference probably proves as much as a large one or a great number. It shows that the teaching of Jesus and of the Essenes was not always the same. The presumption arises then that Jesus was not an Essene, or if he was, he surely would not have been in good standing. How otherwise could he have so openly and explicitly denounced what the Essenes required?

There are more striking differences. The Essenic concept of grading individuals according to hierarchical rank was quite opposite to Jesus' approach to human relationships. We might say that Jesus stated as a principle the ideal of human equality implicit in Essene practice. He resisted every attempt by the disciples to introduce such an element into their circle. "A disciple is not above his teacher," Luke reports him as saying, "but everyone when he is fully taught will be like his teacher."

When the disciples were disputing as to who was going to be the greatest in the heavenly kingdom, he said, "If any one would be first, he must be last of all and servant of all." On one occasion when he observed that those bidden to a feast had appropriated the chief seats for themselves, he said to his disciples, "When you are invited by anyone to a marriage feast, do not sit down in a place of honor, lest a more eminent man than you be invited by him . . . go and sit in the lowest place." When James and John asked if they might sit on his right and left hand in the kingdom, he reiterated his position, "Whoever would be great among you must be your servant."

These sayings are so in contrast to the teachings and practice of the Essenes that again it almost seems as if Jesus had the Essenes in mind. Certainly he knew of the Essene practice. He may have detected in his disciples a liking for the Essene hierarchy and a desire to duplicate it. Possibly some of them had been Essenes. The Manual of Discipline is equally explicit in asserting the principle of protocol. As we have seen, it prescribes that when new members "enter the covenant" "they shall be registered in order, each before his neighbor, according to his understanding and his works, so that everyone of them shall obey his neighbor, the lesser obeying the greater." The members of the order are to undergo "an investigation of their spirits and their works year by year, so as to elevate each one according to his understanding and the perfection of his way, or put him back according to his perversions." In regard to their method of assembly, the Manual says: "This is the order for the session of the masters, each in his position. The priests be seated first and the elders second; then all the rest of the people shall be seated, each in his position."

Another difference between Jesus and the Essenes is to be seen in the fact that Jesus and the disciples were itinerants. "The Son of Man has nowhere to lay his head," said Jesus, but the Essenes lived year after year in their Community House. Josephus says that they dwelt in the chief cities and that they traveled back and forth between them. He may have been mistaken in this, but even if he is correct, the contrast holds between the itinerant who does not know where he is to sleep next and the man who journeys from one known lodging to another.

The asceticism of the Essenes also is in contrast to Jesus' practices. He neither lived apart, nor did he eschew good food and good company. His enemies called him "a glutton and a drunkard." The Son of Man "came eating and drinking," says the Gospel of Matthew. It seems to be plain that the attitude of each toward the good things of life was not the same. The one was strict; the other was permissive.

Much attention has been given to the differences between Jesus and the Essenes in regard to the attitude men are to take toward their enemies. "Love your enemies," says Jesus in the Sermon on the Mount. "Hate all the sons of darkness," says the Manual of Discipline. Many find here a distinctive and final difference between Jesus and the teaching of the Dead Sea Scrolls.

The contrast is great. The terrible curse uttered upon all the men of Belial when the initiate enters the covenant of the Essenes has already been noted. How different are the words of Jesus! "You have heard that it was said, 'You shall love your neighbor and hate your enemy.' But I say to you love your enemies, and pray for those who persecute you. For if you love those who love you, what reward have you? Do not even the tax collectors the same? And if you salute only your brethren, what more are you doing than others? Do not even the Gentiles the same? You, therefore, must be perfect, as your heavenly Father is perfect."

Probably the point at which Jesus and the Essenes were in the most fundamental opposition was in their attitude toward the ancient Law. Both the Pharisees and the Essenes insisted on the strict observance of the old Mosaic Law. Jesus, on the other hand, deliberately broke the Law as it was interpreted by the scribes and Pharisees of his time.

Righteousness was central for Jesus, as it was for the Essenes. But he did not follow the Pharisaical elaborations on the Mosaic Law nor did he accept the literalism which characterizes much of the Essene literature. After saying that he had not come to abolish the Law, but to fulfill it, Jesus said, "I tell you, unless your righteousness exceeds that of the scribes and Pharisees, you will never enter the kingdom of heaven." "Blessed are those who hunger and thirst for righteousness" is one of the Beatitudes. "Seek, first [God's] kingdom and his righteousness," he said, adding that all the material wants of life would follow as a matter of course. Righteousness, not conformity to legal precepts, was his most constant demand.

Jesus showed no patience whatever with the elaborate Sabbath regulations which had been developed in Judaism by the first century A.D. He deliberately healed a man's hand on the Sabbath, although the scribes and Pharisees were watching to see whether or not he would break the rule. "Is it lawful on the Sabbath to do good or to do harm, to save life or to kill?" he asked. He and the disciples plucked ears of grain in violation of the Sabbath also. "The Sabbath was made for man, not man for the Sabbath," he responded when called upon to answer for what they had done.

The contrast with the Essenes on this point too is great. The Manual of Discipline is silent in regard to the Sabbath, but the the Damascus Document stipulates:

"Concerning the Sabbath, to observe it according to its ordinance: Let not a man do work on the sixth day from the time when the sun's disk is its full width away from the gate, for that is what it says: 'Observe the Sabbath day to keep it holy.' And on the Sabbath day let not a man utter anything foolish or trifling. Let him not lend anything to his neighbor. Let them not shed blood over wealth and gain. Let him not speak of matters of work and labor to be done on the morrow. Let not a man walk in the field to do the work of his business on the Sabbath. Let him not walk out of his city more than a thousand cubits. Let not a man eat on the Sabbath day anything but what is prepared. And of what is perishing in the field let him not eat. And let him not drink anything except what is in the camp."

Members of the order are forbidden on the Sabbath to work, to take anything from the house out of doors, to open a sealed vessel, to help an animal in giving birth to the young, or even to lift the young out of a cistern or ditch. Other rules suggest further the severity of Essene law as it relates to the Sabbath. In this regard the Essenes were in harmony with the rest of Judaism. The Sabbath rules in the Torah are no less severe and precise than those recorded in the Damascus Document. Yet all rule following seems to have been foreign to Jesus' nature.

Another matter of fundamental importance in which Jesus and the Essenes seem to have been in sharp disagreement concerns ritualistic cleanliness. The basin for lustration and pools for baptism at the Essene Community Center, offer evidence of the significance of ritualistic washing in Essene thought and practice. Some corroborative evidence is also found in their literature.

The Manual of Discipline speaks of a member sanctifying himself "with water of cleanness" and says that the members "will not be cleansed [by entering the water] unless they have turned from their evil." The Damascus Document reads, "Concerning purification with water: Let not a man. . . ." The remainder, which is brief, sheds little light on the Essene practice.

Jesus' attitude toward things and people said to be "unclean," according to the rules of the Law, was one of outspoken opposition. When a Pharisee invited him to dinner, Jesus accepted. While they were at the table, a woman anointed Jesus' feet with oil. She was a sinner. This means that she was unclean by the standard of Jewish Law. Jesus accepted the tribute of the woman, but the Pharisee could not understand why a "good' Jew would thereby permit himself to become "unclean." On another occasion, Jesus sat at dinner with a group of tax collectors and "sinners." The Pharisees asked the disciples why Jesus permitted himself to be contaminated by eating with people who were unclean.

When the scribes and Pharisees asked him why his disciples flouted the traditions of the elders by eating without first ritualistically washing their hands, he gave a multiple answer. First, he expressed a conviction that such rule-following was an evil because it lacked any religious participation on the part of men who observed the rules. Hence, he argued, it amounted to no more than an empty gesture. He quoted from the prophet Isaiah:

> This people honors me with their lips
> But their heart is far from me
> In vain do they worship me
> Teaching as doctrines the precepts of men.

Then he declared his true criticism of ritual washings. "Hear and understand," he cried, "not what goes into the mouth defiles a man, but what comes out of the mouth, this defiles a man . . . what comes out of the mouth proceeds from the heart . . . evil thoughts, murder, adultery, fornication, theft, false witness, slander. These are what defile a man; but to eat with unwashed hands does not defile a man." Where could we find a sharper contrast with the Essenes and their system of pools and basins and their requirements for ceremonial washing?

We saw his attitude toward oaths as stated in the Sermon on the Mount. It comes out much more clearly in his conflicts with the Pharisees. He called them "blind guides" and "whitewashed tombs, which outwardly appear beautiful, but within they are full of dead men's bones and all uncleanness."

"Woe to you," he cried, "blind guides, who say, 'If any one swears by the temple, it is nothing; but if any one swears by the gold of the temple, he is bound by his oath.' You blind fools! For which is greater, the gold or the temple that has made the gold sacred? And you say, 'If any one swears by the altar, it is nothing; but if any one swears by the gift that is on the altar, he is bound by his oath.' You blind men! For which is greater, the gift or the altar that makes the gift sacred? So he who swears by the altar, swears by it and by everything on it; and he who swears by the temple, swears by it and by him who dwells in it; and he who swears by heaven, swears by the throne of God and by him who sits upon it."

The Pharisees were his constant detractors. They were always on hand to challenge him and to heckle him with questions. And he never failed to meet their challenge. He parried every thrust, turned back every question and was never deterred by them from his chosen course of action. He did not hesitate to acknowledge the importance of the place they held in Judaism. "The scribes and the Pharisees sit on Moses' seat," he said, this referring to the fact that all Israel looked upon them as the fountainhead of the meaning of the Law. Since the Law was fundamental in Israel, no more exalted position could be given to them. Jesus grants this without qualification when he adds, "All therefore whatsoever they bid you observe, that observe and do." To conclude the quotation with these words, however, is completely to distort his thought. "But do not ye after their works, for they say and do not," he continues. The remainder of this fiery passage is a condemnation of the empty observance of rules and of those who, following literal religious precepts, deny the spirit the rules were designed to embody.

The Pharisees, the Essenes and Jesus, as well as the Sadducees, the Zealots and all other elements in Judaism, completely agreed that Yahweh expected his people, bound as they were by the covenant as his chosen people, to follow the Law. The Essenes had gone to the desert, perhaps a century and a half before, because they disagreed with the Pharisees on how the Law was to be observed. The Pharisees, meanwhile, had elaborated upon the written

Law of the Pentateuch with an oral tradition. This we can be sure became distasteful to the Essenes who were conservative and would not tolerate the efforts of anyone to make the Law more reasonable and useful. They felt it must be followed literally exactly as stated. In this Jesus obviously stood with the Essenes. His rebellion against Pharisaic elaborations and distinctions, along with the apparent self-assurance on the part of the Pharisees that they were right, may well reflect Essenic distaste for such temporizing.

There were, on the other hand, two marked differences between the attitude of Jesus and of the Essenes toward the Law. The first is the legalistic attitude evidenced in the Essene literature. The second is in Jesus' statement that he came not to destroy the Law but to fulfill it. This, of course, is what the Essenes believed themselves to be doing. Having concluded that they and not Israel were now the Elect, and that a new covenant now replaced the old one, they looked upon themselves as the new Israel, the inheritors of the ancient covenant of their people. Jesus rejected this claim. He, like John the Baptist, apparently could not believe that this small group of saints who dwelt apart in the Judean desert were God's chosen and would judge the earth when the Messiah should come at the end of days.

The Essenes believed two Messiahs would play a role in these events, a priestly figure, the Messiah of Aaron, and a lay figure, the Messiah of Israel. But as they thought of it, their own role was central also. They as the Lord's Elect were to be the judges of the nations. This of course was most unorthodox and divided them from the Pharisees completely.

Jesus differed from both. He believed in the authority of the Pharisees, but denounced them for empty legalism. His reaction to the legalism of the Essenes seems to have been the same. And yet, while he inveighs bitterly against the Pharisees, he is nowhere recorded as mentioning the Essenes, either by that name or by any other reference we have so far been able to detect. Indeed, the failure of the New Testament to mention the Essenes by name anywhere has given rise to no little speculation.

Jesus seems to have believed that the Law was fulfilled in

himself. He believed the Kingdom was at hand, and that there was little time left in which to repent, a belief that resembles the views of John the Baptist much more than it resembles either that of the Pharisees or that of the Essenes. As he saw it, neither the regulations of Qumran nor the precepts of the Pharisees pointed the way. His fundamental position is plain, whether we turn to his denunciations of the Pharisees or the supreme idealism of the Sermon on the Mount.

By fulfilling the Law he meant getting to the heart of the matter the Law expresses. "Woe to you scribes and Pharisees, hypocrites!" he cried. "For you tithe mint and dill and cummin, and have neglected the weightier matters of the Law, justice and mercy and faith; these ought you to have done, without neglecting the others. You blind guides, straining at a gnat and swallowing a camel!" In the Sermon on the Mount he summed up his views in six vivid contrasts. "Ye have heard that it hath been said by them of old time," he cried. Then he repeated an ancient precept and followed it with these words, "But I say unto you," giving his own version of the matter. Not killing but charity; not adultery but chastity of the mind and heart; not divorce, but constancy; not oaths but honesty; not vengeance but mercy; not hate but love, even of your enemies. Such was his demand. As he saw it, the Law would be fulfilled when men attained ideals such as these. There was not much time. The Kingdom was at hand. The harvest for those who had not repented would be terrible. In his mind the Pharisees had not fulfilled the Law and the New Testament gives us no hint that he thought the Essenes or any similar group had done so either. We are given no intimation that he accepted the Essene doctrine of election. This then is the final distinction between Jesus and the Essenes.

15

THE MEANING OF THE SIMILARITIES AND

DIFFERENCES BETWEEN JESUS AND THE ESSENES

We have found many similarities between Jesus and the Essenes. They are significant and must be accounted for. Yet the differences are so striking that it is impossible to believe that Jesus was an Essene. What then, does the evidence indicate? This for most people is the heart of the Dead Sea Scroll problem.

The attempt to identify Jesus with the Essenes is not new. The discovery of the Scrolls has merely revived and strengthened an idea long familiar to Bible students. Albert Schweitzer in *The Quest of the Historical Jesus* has traced the efforts of men to explain Jesus' life on the theory that he was a secret member of the Essene order. Schweitzer calls these the "imaginary" lives. He tells us that toward the close of the eighteenth century, when rationalism was at its height in Europe, there was a rash of writing in which the Essenes were used to explain the life and work of Jesus of Nazareth.

In Germany about 1790, Karl Bahrdt published a book entitled *An Explanation of the Plans and Aims of Jesus,* in which he accounted for the mysteries in Jesus' life by theorizing that he was the secret agent of the Essenes. About 1800 Karl Venturini, in *Non-Super-Natural History of the Great Prophet of Nazareth,* described the Essenes as behind-the-scenes actors on Jesus' behalf. In 1831 August Gfrorer reached a conclusion, remarkable in the light of what the Dead Sea Scrolls have shown, that the organization of the Christian Church grew out of the organization of the Essene order. He based his surmise on what he was able to glean from Josephus and Philo. Similar works appeared sporadically throughout the nineteenth century. But the Essene theory was given wide circulation in 1863 when the French rationalist, Ernest Renan, published his *Life of Jesus.* The book went through many editions in many languages and was avidly discussed, defended, and refuted for half a century thereafter.

Partly because of insufficient evidence and partly because the Essene hypothesis was distasteful to many people, these speculations fell into disfavor about the turn of the century. At about that time James Moffatt, writing for the *Encyclopedia of Religion and Ethics,* summarily dismissed the Essenes with these words: "They appear and disappear in a mist, leaving hardly a clue to their existence. None of their sacred books has survived. We do not even know whether they were written in Greek or Aramaic. By the time the Rabbinic and Christian literature arose, the literature and almost the very name of the Essenes had vanished from the western world. . . . . At one time attempts were made to trace the affinities of the Essenes with the early Christians and to discover the influence of the former in the ascetic tendencies, the incipient communism, the eschewing of oaths, and the common meals of the primitive churches. But the day for such labors of criticism is over. It is no longer necessary to prove that Jesus was not an Essene and that early Christianity was not Essenic."

Carl Kraeling, a contemporary scholar, published an excellent study of John the Baptist at the time when the Scrolls were first claiming attention. He dismissed the possibility of a connection between the Essenes and John the Baptist as unworthy of examination. He wanted nothing of "earlier theories deriving John's baptism from Essene lustrations" and no "return to the much abused Essenes or the Mystery Cults." This was the position of modern scholarship when the Scrolls were discovered.

From all this literature, we take both courage and caution. The discovery of the Dead Sea Scrolls following upon a century and a half of Biblical criticism has taught us the double lesson of boldness in speculation coupled with the most careful scrutiny of our sources. It has been the boldest spirits who have come nearest to the truth in every case, not those who have been overly cautious. On the other hand, those who have come widest of the mark have been those who were bold but incautious, daring but ignorant or forgetful of the data upon which all knowledge must ultimately rest. Boldness, coupled with exact scholarship, must be our standard too as we seek to extend our knowledge of the Essenes through the Dead Sea Scrolls and to relate their work to the larger context of the world in which they dwelt.

The fatal flaw in every theory that seeks to make Jesus an Essene is that he was baptized by John the Baptist. Of course, some say he was not, but the story of Jesus' baptism by John is about as irreducible a fact as the Gospels relate. Two strong arguments favor its authenticity. First, the story is told by all four Gospel writers, and this can be said of only the most basic narratives in the story of Jesus. Second, the sect of John the Baptist was in the beginning a rival to Christianity. Consequently, because there is a sense in which the baptism seems to make Jesus subservient to John, the story would not have grown up among the followers of Jesus. Accordingly, its presence in the Gospel narratives can be explained only by the fact that it actually happened.

If Jesus had been an Essene, he would have been baptized upon confession, unto the remission of sins, and within the order. As a baptized Essene he would not have felt the need of being baptized by John. If, however, he was among the devout young Israelites who flocked to the Jordan to hear John's preaching, and if, as the Gospels relate, he submitted to baptism along with the rest, we can then explain the similarities between Jesus and the Essenes through John the Baptist, and the differences present no difficulty at all.

The exact nature of the relationship between John and Jesus has long puzzled Bible scholars. In each of the Gospels John appears as a forerunner of Jesus, one who announces his coming. This is the traditional Christian view. Yet scholars have long since detected in the Gospels a different strain of thought. There appears to be more to their relationship than John's prophecy of the coming of the Messiah and the baptism.

The Gospel of Mark, which is the oldest, gives the traditional account in his customarily straightforward manner. John, according to the Gospel of Mark, predicts the coming of one "the thong of whose sandals I am not worthy to stoop down and untie." John further says, "I have baptized you with water, but he will baptize you with the Holy Spirit." Mark then records that John baptized Jesus. We hear nothing more of John until we come to the story of his beheading.

Mark introduces the story of John the Baptist's death almost incidentally. It is the means by which he accounts for Herod's belief that Jesus is John risen from the dead. The same notion, that Jesus is John come to life again, appears in Mark's gospel a second time when Jesus, on the road to Caesarea Philippi, asks the disciples, "Who do men say that I am?" Three answers are offered: John the Baptist, Elijah and one of the prophets. Apparently early in his ministry Jesus was looked upon by some of his followers as one who would appear in the last days, though he is not yet spoken of as the anointed one, the Messiah. The impression from Mark's story is unmistakable that Jesus' ministry began soon after the beheading of John and that at first some people, including Herod, believed he was John risen from the dead. It has long been supposed that John's imprisonment was the impetus for the beginning of Jesus' public ministry. This interpretation conforms to the belief that Jesus was a disciple of John.

The quotation from Luke, given in the chapter on John the Baptist, points up the similarity of John's ethical teaching to that of Jesus and the similarity of his eschatalogy as well. Matthew adds little more. When we turn to the Gospel of John, however, we are in a different climate of opinion. There, as Oscar Cullmann suggests, we seem to have a veritable anti-John-the-Baptist polemic. The evidence which Cullmann offers in support of his view is impressive.

After establishing the fact that Jesus was the Word of God and that he was in the beginning with God, John's Gospel adds:

"And this is the testimony of John, when the Jews sent priests and Levites from Jerusalem to ask him, 'Who are you?' He confessed, he did not deny, but confessed, 'I am not the Christ.' And they asked him, 'What then? Are you Elijah?' He said, 'I am not.' 'Are you the prophet?' And he answered, 'No.' They said to him then, 'Who are you? Let us have an answer for those who sent us. What do you say about yourself?' He said, 'I am the voice of one crying in the wilderness, "Make straight the way of the Lord," as the prophet Isaiah said.' "

It is quite obvious that the author subordinates John to the Anointed One, the Christ. The next paragraph echoes the story as found in the other Gospels. The third and fourth paragraphs reiterate the point. In the fourth paragraph we learn that the earliest of Jesus' disciples were recruited from the disciples of John.

John the Baptist's following did not break up after his death. In fact, during Jesus' lifetime, John's disciples seem to have become a sort of rival sect. From the many evidences of this in the Gospels, Cullmann concludes that the obvious purpose of John's Gospel is to make the primacy of Jesus clear beyond all doubting. He argues that so obvious an effort would not have been necessary if the Baptist's movement had either perished when John was beheaded or had soon thereafter disappeared. Cullmann finds further evidence for his view in the Pseudo-Clementines and the Mandean literature. He believes that the Baptist sect considered John to have been the Messiah, and, consequently, looked upon Jesus as a false Messiah. The warnings against false prophets in John's Gospel have special meaning and purpose in the light of Cullmann's theory. Their obvious purpose seems to have been to strengthen Christian belief that Jesus was the Messiah and to discredit as false prophets all other claimants.

The passages appear in the tenth chapter of John's Gospel. "Truly, truly, I say to you," the Gospel reads, "he who does not enter the sheepfold by the door, but climbs in by another way, that man is a thief and a robber." After explaining how the sheep know their own shepherd, and follow him, the author continues: "A stranger they will not follow but they will flee from him, for they do not know the voice of strangers." Then because the disciples do not understand what Jesus is saying, the Gospel relates, he explains his parable as follows: "Truly, truly, I say to you I am the door of the sheep. All who came before me are thieves and robbers." These, thinks Cullmann, are references to John the Baptist specifically and also to any other of the claimants to Messiahship found in Israel at the time the passage was written.

The language of the First Epistle of John is even stranger. "Children, it is the last hour; and as you have heard that antichrist is coming, so now many antichrists have come. . . . They went out from us but they were not of us for if they had been of us they would have continued with us; but they went out. . . . Who is the liar but he who denies that Jesus is the Christ? This is the antichrist, he who denies the Father and the Son. . . . I write you about those who deceive you. . . . Many false prophets have gone out into the world. . . . They are of the world . . . and the world listened to them. . . . We are of God. Whoever knows God listens to us, and he who is not of God does not listen to us."

Taken by themselves, these passages prove nothing. But taken together with the evidence Cullmann and others have gathered from other parts of the Gospels and other ancient sources, they reveal to us the presence of several Messianic groups in Israel in the early Christian period including that of John the Baptist.

Following his death apparently John's disciples formed a movement and claimed that he had been the Messiah whose coming had long been prophesied in the sacred writings of the Jews.

Likewise, Jesus' disciples, if not during his lifetime, at least soon after his death believed that Jesus was the Messiah. It certainly fits the facts then to surmise that after both had been executed, their respective disciples became rival sects, each with similar teachings derived from a common Essenic and anti-Pharisaic background, each claiming that its own leader had been the Messiah. Judaism naturally denied both claims. When read in the light of this background, the Gospels become clearer and easier to understand, and we can readily see that their purpose is to present an argument, not biography. The Gospels were intended to establish the fact that Jesus had been the Messiah and that as such he would return soon again. This conclusion had been reached by many a scholar long before the Dead Sea Scrolls were discovered.

Another explanation of the differences between Jesus and the Essenes that also accounts for the similarities is the probability that each exhibited a pattern of development and change. Implicit in much of the writing that compares Jesus and the Essenes is the idea that the Essene sect was static throughout its history. Most such writers argue from the Dead Sea Scroll literature as though any document represents what the Essenes believed and practiced throughout the history of the sect.

While it may possibly be true that the sect was as static as this, with much less risk of error it would seem, we may take it for granted that there was development and change among the Essenes. All such groups exhibit patterns of growth and decay. Their teachings and practices rarely remain static. The Manual of Discipline, and the Damascus Document from which most of the contrasts are drawn, apparently antedate the Essene movement as it existed in the time of Jesus by fifty or a hundred years or even more.

While the scholars have striven to accumulate, to analyze, and to explain all the data bearing upon the similarities between Jesus and the Essenes and the differences as well, the theologians have for the most part tended to emphasize the differences and to explain away the similarities. Sometimes the possibility of a connection between the two has been not so much refuted as scoffed at. A typical expression of this point of view is the following paragraph from a review of Geoffrey Graystone's *The Dead Sea Scrolls and the Originality of Christ.*

"Every now and then, there is a flutter among the unbelievers, as a rumor drifts in from the barricades: all is up with Christianity at last. The causes vary: Evolution, relativity, Frazer's *Golden Bough*, but the effects tend to slip into a recognizable pattern. The faith of the non-Christians is profoundly shaken, books are hastily written warning the rest of us to get out while there is still time, the professors abandon us. The agnostics, like so many musical-comedy relatives, wail about how much the patient used to mean to them, and how they will miss him when he's gone."

If the author of the foregoing paragraph had stopped to think about the implications of what he was writing he would have seen that he was proving the validity of the case he attacked. When evolution, relativity, and Frazer's *Bolden Bough* successively made their appearance, churchmen met each one with the same argument this writer now directs at the Dead Sea Scrolls. "Don't get excited," they said. "There is nothing of importance here." But the slowly accumulating evidence on every hand and the slow attrition of decades of close and careful study of all the relevant data have forced the detractors of evolution, of Frazer, and relativity to give in. The position of churchmen in regard to each of these is no longer one of rejection. It is now one of general acceptance.

The author so completely reproduces the familiar pattern, in fact, that he uses against the Dead Sea Scrolls the very argument that was most frequently leveled against evolution. "The theory of evolution cannot be true," it used to be said. "How would you like to be descended from a monkey!" In the same vein it is argued here, "For all their good and creditable by-laws, [the Essenes] condemned their enemies to hellfire. That was the heart of the thing. And if anybody thinks Christianity came from that he can hardly care much whether Christianity survives or not." As we have seen, the curses of the Essenes upon their opponents and the backslidwers from among their own number were by no means "the heart of the thing." Quite apart from the facts in the case, however, this writer apparently does not see that our taste or distaste for Essene practices has no bearing whatever upon the question of the relationship between the Essenes and Jesus.

A different method of explaining away the similarities between Jesus and the Essenes is to say, "This is what we have known all along: the origins of Christianity are Jewish. There is nothing new here!" A typical statement of this point of view is the following from an editorial in *The Living Church:* "Everybody who reads the New Testament knows that baptism was taken over by the Christians from the sect of St. John the Baptist with a new Christian meaning; anyone who has troubled to look into the Eucharistic origins at all, knows that the Holy Communion was originally a rather typical kind of Jewish religious meal, given a new meaning. . . . Christ did not introduce a new morality, a new cosmology or a new rite. What he introduced into all these things was a new Person. . . . There were other Christs—plenty of them. Gamaliel mentions two in the Book of the Acts. . . . The thought that some ancient urn might relaase a genie who will sweep away this movement that Gamaliel's fellow-Jews tried so hard to stamp out . . . is really rather amusing."

To emphasize the Jewishness of early Christianity does not dissociate the Essenes from Jesus, however. It accomplishes the exact opposite. The Judaism out of which Christianity came was not a unity. In the first century A.D., Judaism had many facets, and they were by no means alike. Some of them stand in sharp contrast to each other. Some were bitterly antagonistic. It is almost meaningless to say that the similarities between Jesus and the Essenes all came out of a common Jewish background. They did, even as all the metals known to man were mined from the crust of the earth in which each was embedded. But as we may assume that copper comes from a copper mine and iron from the ore that bears its name, so can we take it for granted that Christianity grew out of the part of Judaism that bears the closest resemblance to it, and from the evidence in the Dead Sea Scrolls, the Essenes appear to have been that part.

In summary, we can certainly say that Jesus and the Essenes were close, although how close we do not know. The similarities are impressive, and among these the expectation of the Messiah must surely be included. On the other hand, most of the differences lose their force when we take into account the close relationship between Jesus and John the Baptist, and the probability of development in the Essene order and in Jesus as well. Though the strictest of the Essenes may have disapproved when he carried their teachings to the multitude and although they undoubtedly criticized his seemingly casual attitude toward the Law, the most perceptive of them could not have failed to see that his teaching flowed out of the mainstream of their heritage.

It was in their tradition that he stood. Whether as a self-proclaimed Messiah or as another of the Lord's prophets, he, like those who had gone before him, called Israel back to her ancient covenant and back to the true worship of Yahweh of Hosts. In him the Law was not destroyed, it was fulfilled.

16

THE SIMILARITIES BETWEEN THE ESSENES AND

THE EARLY CHRISTIAN CHURCH

The evidence for linking the Essene movement with the beginnings of the Christian Church is both voluminous and impressive. This relationship cannot be separated from the relationship between Jesus Christ and the Essenes. The latter question, in turn, cannot be separated from the problem of the historical accuracy of the Gospels. We have seen that the Gospels were written more as polemics than as history. We have also noted that they were written long after the events that they relate. In some cases this time span may have been as much as two or three generations.

If we wish to show that Jesus and the Essenes were closely associated, we need to go further than to the parallels between the New Testament and the Dead Sea Scrolls. We need also to weigh the words that Jesus is quoted as having spoken and also the stories related of him. Every suggested parallel between Jesus and the Essenes may be challenged on the ground that the Gospel record cannot be proved to be historically valid.

This would seem to support a contention that no connection between Jesus and the Essenes can be shown positively to exist.

Yet if the parallels in the Gospels between Jesus and the Essenes do not prove a connection between them, then the parallels must prove a connection between the Essenes and the early church which produced the Gospels. They probably establish a connection with both.

One of the most impressive similarities between the practices of the Essenes and that of the early church is the following passage from Matthew's Gospel: "If your brother sins against you, go and tell him his fault between you and him alone. If he listens to you, you have gained your brother. But if he does not listen, take one or two others along with you, that every word may be confirmed by the evidence of two or three witnesses. If he refuses to listen to them, tell it to the church; and if he refuses to listen even to the church, let him be to you as a Gentile and a tax collector." It has long been questioned whether this passage represents the true words of Jesus, since no "church" existed in his time. Now we know that this passage contains a set of Essene rules which somehow came to be attributed to Jesus sometime before the Gospel of Matthew was written. The same formula is found in the Manual of Discipline and it occurs nowhere else in Judaism.

Such a passage may be used to discredit the alleged parallels between the teachings of Jesus and the teachings of the Essenes, for if these precepts were taken from the Manual of Discipline by the author of the Gospel of Matthew, they were obviously not original with Jesus and cannot be offered as evidence of a connection between Jesus and the Essenes. We are, then, forced to conclude that these precepts were attributed to Jesus by a later writer who must either have been an Essene himself or he must have come under strong Essene influence. How else shall we account for his words? The writer of this passage, the author of Matthew's Gospel, was certainly a member of the early Christian community. It is generally believed that he wrote his Gospel sometime after the destruction of the Temple in A.D. 70. He thus represents the thought of the early Christian Church. The passage makes it clear that he or the sources upon which he drew were close to the Essene sect.

One of the most significant parallels between the Jerusalem church and the Essenes is the manner in which they designated themselves. Just as the Essenes did not speak of themselves as Essenes, so the Christians did not at first speak of themselves as Christians. They were given that name by the people of Antioch who spoke Greek. "Christos" is the Greek equivalent of "Messiah." "Christians" was a natural way for the Greeks to describe the little sect in their midst who believed in an "an anointed one."

Subsequently, Christianity itself adopted the name "Christian." But all this came a long time after the early days in the Jerusalem church. What was their usage then? In the answer to this question lies one of the strongest clues to the relationship between the Essenes and Christian beginnings at Jerusalem. Acts 9:1 records: "Saul, still breathing threats and murder against the disciples of the Lord, went to the high priest and asked him for letters to the synagogues at Damascus so that if he found any belonging to the way he might bring them bound to Jerusalem." The manner of writing makes it clear that the author and his audience know that the people of "the way" are the Christians. No other group in Judaism so characterized itself except the Essenes.

The first Christians thought of themselves as the people of the "New Testament" or "New Covenant." The Essenes thought of themselves as being under a new covenant that had replaced the old covenant between Yahweh and Israel. This concept also is not to be found elsewhere in Judaism. Furthermore, both the Essenes and the Christians describe themselves as "the poor in the world," "the children of light," "the elect of God who shall judge Israel and the nations at the end of days."

A striking similarity is to be found in Luke's much-beloved Christmas story. Scholars have long realized that the angel's song in the King James Version is erroneously translated: "Glory to God in the highest and on earth peace, good will toward men." The translators of the Revised Standard Version replaced these familiar words with the more accurate translation: "Peace on earth among men with whom God is pleased." According to

Frank Cross, the scholars had good reason to believe that an even more accurate translation would read: "Peace on earth among men of God's favor," or "among those who, by God's gracious election, find themselves members of the eschatalogical community." These scholars now know they were right, for the same phraseology appears in the Manual of Discipline. It appears nowhere else in Judaism, and it is clear from the context that its meaning is that given in the last of the translations above.

So striking are conceptual parallels between the Essenes and the earliest Christians that a case for connecting the two movements may be made on this basis alone. Discussing the Dead Sea Scrolls, Cross says: "We are in the conceptual world of the New Testament. The New Testament and Essene writers draw on common resources of language, common theological themes and concepts, and share common religious institutions. They breathe the same atmosphere, confront the same problems. We can now enter into this rich, variegated world of sectarian Judaism in the first century with new boldness and understanding; the strange world of the New Testament becomes less baffling, less exotic. We know better the connotation of its foreign idiom: powers and principalities, flesh, 'to do truth,' sanctification, the poor, men of favor; we can understand why some views and institutions and ideas were discarded and others borrowed, validated or transformed."

A remarkable similarity between the Essenes and the early church is seen in their peculiar use of Old Testament prophecy. It is true that in no New Testament book do we find pesher of the type we see in the Habakkuk Commentary or in the Commentary on Psalm 37. Its equivalent, however, is to be found in the insistence of the Gospel writers that the Scripture was fulfilled in certain events in Jesus' life. This point of view, present in all the Gospels, may be said to dominate the Gospel of Matthew. Krister Stendahl holds that Matthew's Gospel was produced in a "school" of converts to Christianity which desired to find predictions of events in Jesus' life in the Old Testament.

Jesus' birth, according to Matthew, was foretold by Isaiah and the site of Bethlehem was foretold by Micah. Herod's massacre of the children is found in Jeremiah; the return from Egypt in Hosea; the coming of John, the mission in Galilee, the miracles of healing and Jesus' avoidance of publicity in Isaiah. The prediction that Jesus would preach in parables is found in the Psalms; the inability of the people to understand the meaning of his words in Isaiah; his entry into Jerusalem as King in Zechariah. Jeremiah provided the authors with many of the prophecies connected with Jesus' death.

The members of the Jerusalem church looked upon the sacred writings of the Jewish people in exactly the same manner as did the Essenes. They, and indeed all Israel, regarded the Old Testament as sacred. But here, too, there was a difference in which the Essenes and the Christians were like each other. The Old Testament canon had been virtually closed for perhaps two hundred years, although not officially until the Council of Jamnia in A.D. 90. In the first decades of the Christian Era, therefore, the books that were regarded as divinely inspired had long been differentiated from those that were not. Yet there were a number of other books which were considered as sacred by many individual Jews. They belonged to the pseudepigrapha. Both the Christians and the Essenes made considerable use of this extra-biblical literature.

It is also interesting to note that both groups made the most use of the same Old Testament books. For example, in the fragment literature there are thirteen fragments from Deuteronomy, thirteen from Isaiah and ten from the Psalms, as well as a lesser number from other Old Testament books. These same books, Deuteronomy, Isaiah and Psalms, figure most prominently in the New Testament.

There are many similarities between the Gospel of John and the Dead Sea Scrolls. John's Gospel, generally thought to be the latest of the four, dating perhaps from A.D. 90, is now thought to reflect the viewpoint of at least one part of the Christian Church in its formative period. Many of the similarities between this Gospel and the Scrolls have no particular significance when taken separately because the same elements are found elsewhere in Judaism. Nevertheless, they have cumulative weight when added to a body of evidence that is distinctive of Essenism and Christianity. Many elements in John's Gospel are distinctive to these two movements only.

Lucetta Mowry in her study of the relationship of the Gospel of John and the Dead Sea Scrolls points to several of these elements. There is in the Fourth Gospel, for example, the dualism or division of the world into light and darkness, matter and spirit, good and evil. This, like the dualism of the Dead Sea Scrolls, she believes was derived ultimately from Iranian dualism and the religion of Zoroaster. The Essenic and Christian views differ from the Iranian view in the same manner. In Zoroastrianism the struggle between Ahura Mazda and Ahriman, light and darkness, was originally an even contest in which the final victory was unknown. For the Essenes and the Christians the issue was never in doubt; God would win. As creator of the forces of both darkness and light, he is supreme. Such dualism never had a conspicuous place in orthodox Judaism.

Much discussion has centered in the concern of the Essenes for the ancient Jewish calendar. The Manual of Discipline and the Damascus Document stress the importance of observing festivals at the proper times. Although the details of the matter have not yet been worked out, all agree that holding to the old Israelitic calendar was a conviction of the Essenes and a point of contention with Judaism. Professor Mowry finds in the Gospel of John an equally great emphasis upon the Jewish sacred calendar which is there integrated into the work of Jesus. This, if true, is a striking parallel because of its contrast to the rest of Judaism. Insistence upon clinging to the old calendar seems to have been one of the points on which the Essenes first divided from the religion of Israel.

The most arresting parallels are found in the comparison of the Essene movement and the structure of the Jerusalem church. The consensus today is that the Jerusalem church was gathered under the leadership of Peter. Either before or shortly after the crucifixion of Jesus, Peter and the other disciples came to believe that he had been the Messiah and that he would return again soon. The belief in his second coming undoubtedly came after he had passed from the human scene. This fully developed

Messianic conviction was far more complete than that of the Essenes.

Soon others began to join with them. All were Jews, and as we have seen, they differed with their fellow countrymen only in believing that the long-expected Messiah had already come. The practice of admitting Gentiles was not adopted until some time after when their movement had begun to spread through Asia Minor. Any Gentile who desired to join the Jerusalem group had first to become a proselyte, that is to say, a convert to Judaism. It is with these men, the earliest believers in Jesus as the Messiah, that we are here primarily concerned. They constituted what the Book of Acts refers to as the Church at Jerusalem. At the outset such organization as developed among the disciples probably amounted to little more than a new and separate synagogue in Israel's ancient capital. Except for the fact that its members were given to speaking in tongues and exhibited various other evidences of spiritual seizure, the group at first probably attracted little attention.

A number of scholars believe that the General Epistle of James gives a vivid picture of the Jerusalem church at its beginning. Theodore Gaster, a leading exponent of the position, writes, "It is now generally agreed that this document, addressed to 'the twelve tribes in the dispersion,' was written between 40 A.D. and 50 A.D., that its author was James, the 'brother' of Jesus, who occupied a leading position among the Jewish Christians in Jerusalem (Acts 12:17; 15:13; 21:18); and that it represents the outlook of what has been called 'the church of the circumcision'—that is, the circle of Jews who were ready to accept the general teachings of Jesus and his call to regeneration but were not prepared to view them through the prism of Pauline philosophy and doctrine." Professor Gaster then gives several examples of ideas and expressions that are common to the Epistle of James and the Qumran texts. He concludes "that the Dead Sea Scrolls [may] open a window upon the little community of Jewish Christians clustered around James in Jerusalem."

Sherman E. Johnson, who has studied the relationship of the fledgling Christian Church at Jerusalem and the Essenes at

Qumran, says that the author of the Luke-Acts seems to be greatly interested in the Jewish origins of the new way, although he himself wrote for a Gentile audience. Apparently he was well-informed about the Jerusalem church. That church, as seen in the early chapters of Acts, Johnson argues, is reminiscent of the Qumran sect.

There appears to be ample evidence to support Johnson's contention. In the first place, the Jerusalem church was founded as a result of the experience of the disciples at Pentecost, where, they believed, the Holy Spirit visited them. They believed that all who repented and were baptized received the Spirit. The Essenes, according to the Manual of Discipline, thought they, too, possessed the Spirit. They held that it cleanses men from sin and that the spirit of truth is sprinkled on a man like water. The Essenes practiced baptism in some form a rite also practiced by the early Christians. Both led lives of communal sharing, and both regarded poverty as holy.

Another of the more arresting similarities between the earliest Christian community and the Essene sect was that each was governed by twelve men. Of course, Jesus had twelve disciples and the twelve tribes of Israel provide the prototype for the use of the number twelve wherever it occurs, as it frequently does, in Israel's thought. Nevertheless, there is more to the "twelve" as we see it in Acts than this. Johnson points out that until the discovery of the Dead Sea Scrolls, it had never been quite clear why the disciples needed to appoint a twelfth apostle to take the place of Judas. But if twelve men constituted the community's council, then the reason is clear.

What is more remarkable is that these twelve, according to early Christian thought, appear to have the same role to play in the time of Messianic expectation that the Essenes assigned to their rulers. The Gospel of Luke reports Jesus as saying to the twelve, "I appoint for you that you may eat and drink at my table in my kingdom and sit on thrones judging the twelve tribes of Israel." The parallel to the language in the Manual of Discipline at this point is close.

It is unnecessary to list all the parallels between the Essene community and the earliest Christian community. The more impressive of those that remain ought, however, to be noted. A number of priests were active and loyal members of both the Essene and Christian groups. We have noted the similarity between the communal meals at Qumran and those of the Christians. Both speak of the "tabernacle" of David rather than of the Temple. To speak of the "Temple" was common usage in Israel at the time of the early Christians. "Tabernacle," an archaic term was the kind of usage which isolated conservatives like the Essenes would tend to preserve.

It is generally agreed that the stoning of Stephen was a crucial event in the life of the Jerusalem church. Among the leaders of the movement, Stephen appears to have been one of the greatest. When he was seized and dragged before the Sanhedrin, the fate of the followers of Jesus was sealed. So fiery and denunciatory was his speech before that august body that "they cried out with a loud voice and stopped their ears and rushed together upon him. Then they cast him out of the city and stoned him."

Their fury was not without justification. "You stiff-necked people, uncircumcised in heart and ears," Stephen had said to them, "you always resist the Holy Spirit. Which of the prophets did not your fathers persecute? And they killed those who announced beforehand the coming of the Righteous One, whom you have now betrayed and murdered, you who received the Law as delivered by angels and did not keep it."

The resemblance of his words to the Essene point of view is too striking to be denied. The Manual of Discipline has a similar metaphorical reference to uncircumcision. We have noted the Essene use of the concept of the Spirit. We know of their expectation and predictions of the coming of the Messiah. On the basis of these similarities Johnson suggests that Stephen may himself have been an Essene, or that, at the least, he represents an Essene influence in the Jerusalem church.

Johnson further suggests that the passages in Matthew, which are not duplicated in Mark or Luke, may also represent the tradition of the Jerusalem church. These contain ideas of perfection in personal life which, duplicating the Essenic ideal, go beyond the Pharisaic ideal of scrupulously following the Law. In them the Pharisees are criticized severely. The regulation about offending brothers, found also in the Manual of Discipline, is included in these passages.

In the structure of the Christian community, as we see it in the Book of the Acts, are to be found the most interesting parallels. The assembly of the members of the Essene community, known as "the Many," was the central governing body of the order. Scholars point out that behind the numerous translations of both the Scrolls and the New Testament there is a single word of which "the Many" is now recognized as the best translation. It was "the Many" at Jerusalem who, in the dispute over the circumcision of converts, kept silent and listened to Paul and Barnabas when they related what signs and wonders God had done through them. It was "the Many" at Antioch who heard the letter Paul and others brought. And it was "the Many" whom the Twelve assembled for the appointing of seven assistants. The "Many" is the ecclesia, or assembly of the New Testament from which our word "ecclesiastic" is derived. Only here, it is pointed out, only among the early Christians and the Essenes does the word for "the Many" refer to the type of democratic assembly with governing powers which the Book of the Acts and the Manual of Discipline set so clearly before us.

The parallels in the practice of communion are startling. The following is from the fragment Scroll literature. "When they solemnly meet at the table of communion, or to drink the wine, and the communion table is arranged and the wine is mixed for drinking, one shall not stretch out his hand on the first portion of bread or on the wine before the Messiah-Priest; for he shall bless the first portion of the bread and the wine, and stretch out his hand on the bread first of all. Afterwards the Messiah of Israel shall stretch forth his hands on the bread; and after giving a blessing all the congregation of the Community shall partake each according to his rank.

"And they shall follow this prescription whenever the meal is arranged, when as many as ten meet together."

The love feast of the Essenes had a symbolic quality. It was a meal that friends, united in a common cause, enjoy together and it was symbolically a representation of a banquet to be held by the Essenes and their two Messiahs, the Messiah of Aaron and the Messiah of Israel, at the end of days. Such a symbolic meal, says Frank Cross, to whom we are indebted for pointing to this parallel, is exactly duplicated in the New Testament.

"In the Markan account," he says, "it appears in the words, 'Truly I say to you, I shall not drink again of the fruit of the vine until that day when I drink in the kingdom of God' (14:25). In the Lukan version it is even stronger, especially if one follows the shorter text (Luke 22:14-19a); and it is found as well in the Pauline and later formulas; 'For as often as you eat this bread and drink the cup, you proclaim the Lord's death *until he comes.*'"

Here then is some of the evidence that indicates a close connection between the Essenes and the first Christians. What do these facts mean for us?

17

The Meaning of the Similarities between

the Essenes and the Early Christian Church

The differences between the early Christian Church at Jerusalem and the Essene sect at Qumran are so obvious no one has proposed that the Jerusalem church was, in effect, an Essene community. These differences include, among others, all the differences between Jesus and the Essenes already noted; the isolation at Qumran contrasted with the Christian community in the midst of urban Jerusalem; the belief of the Christians that they and not the Essenes were the Elect; and most conspicuously the expectation of the two Messiahs at Qumran as against the profound conviction among the Christians that in the person of Jesus of Nazareth the Messiah had already come.

The amazing similarities between the two movements, however, apart from the obvious differences, raise a profound question in the minds of all of us. Clearly there was a close connection between them. What was it?

Unfortunately, the Scrolls have not as yet provided us with an answer to this question. As in the case of Jesus, it is not to be expected that we shall find in the Essene literature references to

the Christian Church at Jerusalem, even if we grant a close connection between the two. The Scrolls were written too early. The
literary evidence of a connection between the two movements
must all go the other way. We shall have to look for such evidence
of a connection as may exist in the literature of the Christians.

There are, however, two clear indications of a connection
between the Jerusalem church and the Qumran community of
a nonliterary character. The first of these is the fact of the relationship between Jesus and the Essenes. The Messiah in whom the
Jerusalem church believed appears either to have been an Essene
himself at one time or to have been greatly influenced by them,
probably through John the Baptist. In the light of these circumstances, is it not almost a foregone conclusion that a close relationship would have continued between his followers and the
Essenes? We are baffled here by an almost total lack of information, and forced to rely upon inference. But is not such an
inference sound when there is so much else to corroborate it?

A second and far more definite indication that these two movements interacted upon each other is their geographical proximity
to each other. For a period of forty years, from perhaps A.D. 30
to 70, the Essenes occupied the Community Center at Qumran
while the Christian Church was developing at Jerusalem. Of
course, simple geographical proximity proves nothing. Many
movements exist side by side over a long period of time, without
having the slightest influence upon one another. But here we are
confronted with a great many similarities which suggest interdependence, and a geographical proximity which made close
contact possible.

During the years when the two communities stood but two days'
journey apart, would not members of the one from time to
time visit the other? If John the Baptist was an Eessene who
wanted to take the Essene teaching to all Israel, it it not likely
that other members of the group might have left Qumran to
join him or Jesus or the apostles in Jerusalem? Is it not also
likely that there were Essenes who felt a strong sense of spiritual
kinship with Jesus? Having known him and his work, might not
some of them have believed with the apostles that he was indeed

the Messiah whose coming had been foretold in Israel's ancient Scriptures? Would not some of them join the rest of the believers at Jerusalem? Do not the many similarities and the geographical proximity of the two groups make all these things possibilities?

One of the aspects of the Jerusalem church that has long puzzled scholars is the organizational skill of the "uneducated men" who had been the followers of Jesus. The structure of the first Christian community was amazingly efficient and strong. The internal dissensions were handled as they came up with dispatch and dexterity and differences of opinion were quickly ironed out. The recalcitrant were sternly dealt with. Meanwhile, the community grew and prospered.

This organizational know-how of the first Christians came from the Essenes, for all the institutional problems faced by the first Christian Church in Jerusalem had been met and solved by the Essenes in the hard pragmatic school of experience that extended back for a period of some hundred and fifty years. At Jerusalem, during the reign of Herod the Great, the Essenes had, in a great and largely hostile city, held a group of people to a common loyalty and to a religious ideal. This the Christians were now attempting to do. The organization, structure, rules of conduct, including initiation and expulsion of members, and order of worship and sacrament, had been worked out for them by the Essenes. Even the beliefs, except for the belief as to whether the Messiah had come, were already agreed upon. The Christian Church had only to appropriate for its own use the main elements of the Essene movement and then to add its own special emphases and interpretations, chief of which was the belief that Jesus was the Messiah for whom Israel had been waiting.

Nevertheless, during the time that the Christian Church was growing at Jerusalem and the Essene sect continued on at Qumran, they would have been rival movements in spite of their many similarities and interrelationships. Unless the Manual of Discipline had been given up as the code of conduct for the brotherhood, any Essene who left the sect to join with James and Peter at Jerusalem would have been cursed as an apostate. It is possible that the Jerusalem church was an Essene branch, but we have seen the enormous difficulties lying in the way of such a supposition. Thus whatever direct influence came into the Jerusalem church from Qumran, came from Essenes who were forced to desert the order and to become apostates if they were to become a part of the Christian community.

We can make the further assumption that the Qumran community had by this time lost much of the fluidity that characterized it at the outset. Its rules, which initially had been a means to an end, had by this time doubtless become ends in themselves. The sect throughout its history was characterized by rigidity. It was the inflexibility of the founders in their interpretation of the ancient Law that had driven them into the desert in the first place. In the light of what we know of similar groups, are we not justified in concluding that the Essenes in this period had become an intransigent community of legalists, quite at variance with the burgeoning Christian movement at Jerusalem? Yet can we not also assume that such legalism would have elicited its own protest among the Essenes? Is it not likely that some of the men who were initially drawn to these desert ascetics because of their holiness, might later have been repelled by their legalism and their exclusive messianism as well. If this had happened might not some of these men have sought the answer to their spiritual needs among the Christians? Thus the influence of the Essenes on the Christians would have been great, while the influence of the Christians on the Essenes would have been almost nil, which is exactly what such records as we possess indicate.

It is in this sense, perhaps more than any other, that Christianity is an outgrowth of the Essene sect. Theologically Christianity was a spiritualization of Essenism, as Essenism had been a spiritualization of Pharisaism. Psychologically it took its rise from the conviction that Jesus of Nazareth was in fact the Messiah. Sociologically and ecclesiastically, Christianity adopted many essential forms, the structure and practices of the Essenes. These were important factors which enabled Christianity to survive.

Of course, organizational experience is not an adequate explanation of the origin of the Christian Church. Neither is a supposed revolt against increasing Essene legalism. Essene know-how does not explain why the followers of Jesus eventually won out over the followers of John the Baptist or over any of the other of the competing Messianic groups. The followers of both Jesus and John had close connections with the Essenes. The difference, then, must be found in the two men, in their lives, in their teachings, and in the quality of followers they were able to draw about them. The data that has come to us through the Dead Sea Scrolls, together with the information we already possessed, leads to the conclusion that in the person of Jesus is to be found the explanation of Christianity's special qualities.

It is for this reason that Christian faith is not likely to be upset as a result of the discovery of the Dead Sea Scrolls. Christian faith has always centered in the person of Jesus of Nazareth. This faith has been stated variously but all have agreed that the position of Jesus in the Christian religion is central. The data disclosed by the Scrolls in no way contradicts this appraisal. Quite apart from the surmise that faith has made, what we can learn historically of the life of the Nazarene through the Dead Sea Scrolls underscores the estimate Christians have always made as to his significance. The facts in this case support faith.

The theological arguments of the scholars have, on the other hand, sometimes led to an opposite conclusion. Apparently out of the desire to show that Christian faith is not affected by the Scroll finds, certain scholars have insisted not only that nothing in the Scrolls has affected Christian faith but that nothing they might be found to contain could do so. For example, in a theological addendum to an excellent summary of the knowledge so far gathered about the Scrolls, Walter Harrelson of the Chicago Divinity School asks rhetorically, "Does [the Scroll data] mean that Christianity is a kind of Essenism, a religious development directly out of the Dead Sea community? Few scholars would say so on the basis of the available evidence," he answers, and how true his appraisal is, we have seen in the preceding pages.

But Dean Harrelson continues, not satisfied to rest his case on the evidence. "This is not, however, because Christians have anything to fear or to regret, should such prove to be the case. The New Testament declares that, in Jesus Christ, God fulfilled his promise to the fathers of old. . . . The Community of the Covenant awaited the coming of the Messiah; the New Testament Community affirmed in faith that he had come."

Thus the theological position seems to be that belief in Jesus as the Messiah distinguished the Christians from all other contemporary sects. This may be theologically accurate: who is to say when a theology is right and when it is wrong? Factually considered, however, such a statement is incorrect. "The community of the Covenant awaited the coming of the Messiah," says the Dean. "The New Testament community affirmed in faith that he had come—although in an entirely different way from what was generally expected." But so did the followers of John the Baptist, and so did perhaps half a dozen other sects with Messianic claims that sprang up in that period in Israel. Each affirmed in faith that the Messiah had come in a way other than the expected, and that their particular leader was he.

Consequently, on the basis of the theological argument, we are left with no distinction between the movement that followed John's work and that which ensued upon the work of Jesus. If the distinction is a claim based upon such an article of faith, then Christianity is reduced to the status of one of the several Messianic groups in first-century Israel, each of which made bold to proclaim that its leader was the Messiah come upon earth. If, however, we leave out the theology and stick to the data history provides, and if we continue to be exacting when we accept data as valid or reject it as invalid, then we come out with the conclusion that has always been central in Christianity —namely, that Jesus Christ towers above his contemporaries because of what he *was,* not because of what people *thought* he was. The beliefs *about* him stemmed from the kind of person he *was.* The man explains the beliefs about him; the beliefs do not explain the man. Jesus is not made unique because of what people believed about him then or what they believe about him now. The uniqueness we find in him is his own. It shines out of his own character.

Another way to state the point is this. It is arguing in a circle to say that Christianity is unique because Jesus' followers believed he was unique and wrote their belief into the New Testament. Their belief does not establish the fact. The fact is the means by which we test the validity of belief, not vice versa.

To employ this theological argument in a discussion of the Dead Sea Scrolls gives the case away to the opposition. There was very little that was unique about the beliefs of the apostles at the outset. A careful study of even the meager data we possess makes this quite clear. The early beliefs of the apostles were simply characteristic of the beliefs of other millennialist groups in Israel at the time. The apostles differed from the others only in that they centered their belief in one individual while competing sects centered their beliefs in others.

In spite of all the effort that has been expended to that end, Christians do not now, and they probably never will, think alike about the person of Jesus Christ. They need have no fear, however, that the Dead Sea Scrolls will destroy the one thing upon which they do think alike—namely, the central place of Jesus of Nazareth has always had in their thought and in their faith. But this is true for factual reasons coming out of a study of the Scrolls, not for the theological reasons usually given. It is true because the new body of data that has come into our hands through the Scrolls confirms the experience of the first Christians, and the experience of Christianity down the years since that time.

This is the crux of the matter. The discovery of the Dead Sea Scrolls is important to us because of the light it throws on the origin of our religion. It is doubly important because it further confirms the position Christians have always held regarding Jesus Christ. They enable us to see more clearly than we have ever been able to see before, that our faith is grounded in fact rather than fancy—that Christianity comes to us through him and because of him, and that without the stamp of his peculiar genius upon it, the movement might in truth have been but

another Essenism, or another sect like that of John the Baptist
or Theudas or Judas of Galilee.

As time went on the Essene colony and the Jerusalem church
must surely have drawn further apart. The convictions of the
Christians which became increasingly central in this period—that
Jesus was the Messiah—could not have been congenial to the
Essenes. They expected two Messiahs. Furthermore, Jesus had
not brought about the cataclysmic end that the Essenes, together
with most of the rest of Israel, expected the Messiah to produce.
As the stoning of Stephen marks the beginning of the persecution
of the Jerusalem church by the Jews, it also marks the beginning
of the mission to the Gentiles. We know of the increasing rift
in the Jerusalem church on this matter. By seeking to exclude
Gentiles, it ultimately lost its position of leadership among the
Christian churches. The intransigence of the Jerusalem church
toward Gentiles doubtless reflects the far greater rigidity of the
Essenes on the question.

When the end came at Qumran, however, the qualities the
Essenes are known to have possessed must have stood out at their
best. In the following passage Josephus does not say that he is
describing their demise, but at least his words are applicable, for
they suggest to us the scene that marked the end of the Essene
colony at the hands of the Emperor Vespasian and the Tenth
Roman Legion. Josephus wrote:

"They make light of danger and triumph over pain by their
resolute will; death, if it comes with honor, they consider better
than immortality. The war with the Romans tried their souls
through and through by every variety of test. Racked and
twisted, broken and burnt, and made to pass through every in-
strument of torture in order to induce them to blaspheme their
Lawgiver or eat some forbidden thing, they refused to yield to
either demand, nor ever once did they cringe to their persecutors
or even shed a tear. Smiling in their agonies and mildly deriding
their tormentors, they cheerfully resigned their souls, confident
that they would receive them back again."

The Jerusalem church fell two years later when the Romans
under Vespasian's son Titus destroyed the city in A.D. 70. Un-

daunted, the members withdrew across the Jordan, where they became the Jewish-Christian sect known to history as the Ebionites, a name that means "the poor." There are remarkable similarities between the thought and character of the Ebionites and the Essenes, although there are some differences also. Perhaps some of the Essenes joined the Jerusalem church in Jordan at that time.

In any case, all the evidence we have seems to indicate that by A.D. 70, Christianity and Essenism had already moved some distance apart. The Essene sect was Jewish and remained so in spite of its differences with official Judaism, while Christianity, under the leadership of Paul, became a Gentile sect. The same rigorous discipline that characterized the Essene movement throughout its history, its strict observance of the Law and of its own ceremonial, its habit of living apart—all these were abandoned by the Christian Church.

In fact, if we could see back into those ancient days, we might well find that, the Essene movement became more and more ingrown as time went on, and that as its rules multiplied and its rule-keeping became more central, the spirit rather than the letter of its great traditions was carried on more by the Christians at Jerusalem than by the Essenes themselves. There is a very close parallel between the experience of the Pharisees who first separated from their fellow Pharisees back in the time of John Hyracanus, and the experience of the first Christians at Jerusalem, For the earlier period we have little on which to go, but the details of the later period suggest what the earlier one may have been like. The Book of Acts shows the early Christians constantly in conflict with the authorities of official Judaism. They continually got into trouble with the Sanhedrin because they would not keep still. They felt compelled to preach their convictions and did so. We can see from the Scroll Psalms that in like manner the early Essenes were constantly in trouble with the authorities of Judaism in their day and for the same reason. They would not keep still either. They, too, felt compelled to preach what they believed, and did so. We have every reason to believe that their utterances were much like those of Stephen.

Jesus might say, "O Jerusalem that killeth the prophets." For him it was the dreadful truth. But the fate of Jesus and John and probably the Teacher of Righteousness is not typical. Neither is that of Stephen. We should not forget Gamaliel the Pharisee, who rose in the Sanhedrin to demand that Peter be permitted to speak, however much he troubled the Jerusalem community. "Let these men alone," said Gamaliel, "for if this plan or this undertaking is of men, it will fail; but if it is of God, you will not be able to overthrow them. You might even be found opposing God!" Gamaliel represents the ancient and authentic tradition in Israel out of which the whole prophetic movement rose. In accordance with it, five centuries of prophets were permitted a very real "freedom of speech" in Israel, and the earliest of the Essenes went unmolested in the time of John Hyrcanus. It was such tolerance as this, a tolerance that permitted those with whom the authorities profoundly disagreed, that made the prophetic, the Essene and the Christian movements possible.

In modern parlance we call leave to be heard "freedom of speech." But the principal in accordance with which these men were permitted to speak was quite a different one. Their concepts were all theological. Israel came to believe early in her history that God speaks directly to men. For this reason the Israelites believed that a "man of God" must be permitted to speak, no matter how unpalatable his words might be. The chief difference between the earlier and the later day was the fact that the prophets spoke in the name of the Lord while, excepting Jesus, the men of later times did not. It is this single doctrine above all others that is the key to Israel's greatness. She did not slay the Lord's prophets as the princes and priests of other nations were accustomed to do. In the great prophetic period she let them be heard and, to a lesser degree, in the later period also. Because the prophets of Israel were heard, their words made an impact upon the people that eventually shaped Israel's character as a nation, and subsequently the character of the Western world.

This one factor molded Israel's destiny above all others, and out of it her native religious genius flowed. The Essenes inherited the benfits that came to Israel as a result of it. When the

Hasmoneans repudiated the ancient tradition, the Essenes withdrew from the religion and culture of their people in order to sustain it. In the desert, unhampered and alone, they continued the tradition that the Lord is ever nigh to his own, that he speaks to them, that they who hear his voice must give voice to what they hear, and that with unswerving allegiance they must follow his will and his way.

18

Prophets in the Great Tradition

*

The significance of some of the great events in history is
recognized when they occur, but some of the greatest are almost
unnoticed by contemporaries. Men could see that the history
of Rome changed when Julius Caesar crossed the Rubicon. His
act brought to an end the great republic of Rome, and the empire
took its place. But when a Galilean preacher, who claimed to be
the Messiah, was crucified in Jerusalem some seventy-five years
later, only a few believers took notice.

Which was the greater event is no longer questioned. It is now
clear that in the days of Julius Caesar the old Roman republic
was crumbling and that whether he had crossed the Rubicon or
not, the empire would have replaced the dying republic. But the
profound effect upon subsequent history of the crucifixion of
Jesus admits of little dispute.

Did those who saw the crucifixion of Jesus imagine that they
were witnessing an event, the importance of which would be
taken for granted two thousand years later? And which of the
citizens of Jerusalem, who watched the little band of Essenes
make its way out of the city, supposed that their going would
influence the lives and thoughts of men for centuries afterward?
Now in the light of the Scroll discoveries we know that their
exodus was fraught with significance for the future.

Least of all did the Essenes themselves consider their actions to be important. The greatest deeds in the annals of men seldom are done self-consciously. They are done out of necessity and conviction and because at the moment there seems to be no alternative. Conviction makes one demand; society makes another. In the attempt to resolve the conflict, weak men surrender, foolish men become vainglorious, and strong men suffer and often die. It was just such a conflict in which the Essenes were involved when they went out into the desert. There was nothing of the dramatic in their decision and there were no heroics about their departure. They were not trying to prove something to themselves or to the people of Jerusalem. They were simply leaving an unfriendly city whose indifference to their teachings they could not tolerate, a city which in its turn was becoming increasingly intolerant of them.

And yet there was a dimension to the thought of the Essenes that gave their departure a sense of transcendent importance in their own eyes. Their departure was animated by an overarching sense of purpose—namely, the keeping of the covenant between Yahweh and Israel. Theirs was an act of desperation rising out of a profound conviction. All Judea agreed with them that the Law must be observed. But the Essenes believed it must be kept in particular and special ways, or it was not really kept at all. It was their determination to keep the Law in this strict fashion that gave their decision both dignity and purpose. There is perhaps a sense in which they fled into the desert, but it would be much more accurate to say that they went in order to live by a conviction that seemed to them to be all-important.

In so doing, the Essenes aligned themselves with one of the greatest human traditions—that which calls upon man to remain loyal to what he believes even though the authorities of religion or government or both oppose him with determination and violence. In the choice they made, they stood with the greatest leaders of their own people, with Amos and Isaiah, with Jeremiah, with Micah, and with Jesus of Nazareth.

But they stood also in yet wider company. In the steadfastness with which they held and continued to speak aloud their convictions regardless of the persecution and threats of those in authority, the Essenes took their place with Xenophanes and Socrates in Greece, with Peter in Jerusalem, with Paul in Asia Minor, and with the Christian martyrs who died in the arenas of Rome. They took their place also with Peter Waldo and John Wycliffe, John Hus, Martin Luther, and a host of the early leaders of the Reformation. With them, too, stand the Anabaptists, and the English Separatists and Puritans who went into the wilderness that was America when their religious conscience could not be squared with the forms and ceremonies of the Church of England.

The Essenes, like their spiritual counterparts in many ages and many lands, were animated by a vision of holiness. They saw their vision in terms of the concepts that prevailed in their day. The strength of their vision and its power to command their loyalty was derived from the vitality of the religion in which they were nurtured. As the great tradition of independent thinking in Hellas animated Socrates and as the great tradition of piety in the Roman Church animated Luther, so the determination of the Children of Israel to follow the Law of the Lord and to keep the covenant as his Elect was the spiritual force that animated the Essenes.

If we are to judge by the Dead Sea Scrolls, the Essenes were possessed of the same fierce passion for holiness that characterizes the history of Israel as far back as the time of the prophet Elijah. They withdrew from the world to save themselves. They did not withdraw to the wilderness of Judea because of a desire to live in isolation from the ways of commerce and society. We find them at Qumran because only in the desert could they follow the Law of the Lord as they believed that they and all Israel ought to do.

The desert rewarded them well for the choice they made. In the midst of its desolation they found the opportunity to follow the Law and to keep the covenant as the remnant of the Lord's Elect. There, untroubled by men whose vision was less clear, they worshiped the Lord and meditated in his Law day and night. In the forbidding environs of the wilderness they found the privation they expected, and as we have seen, they found much more besides. The isolation and hardship of the desert drew them together in an intimate fellowship. The disciplines they were required to fashion and to enforce in order to make their community life run smoothly, the separation from the formal Temple worship of their fathers and the necessity for justifying their separate existence—all these forces taken together made of the Essenes a most unusual type of social unit.

In the extraordinary development which took place during the two centuries the Essene movement flourished at Qumran, the desert played its own special part. It was to one of the most desolate spots in all the earth that they went. The flat plain that rims the Dead Sea, and the bleak hills that rise about it, offer as forbidding a prospect as one might hope to see anywhere. Nothing grows there except in the spring when there is a little rainfall. The ground is as hard and as lifeless as a city playground and not a tree or a bush obstructs the view in any direction. At Qumran, there are only the hills of Judea in the west, the hills of Moab in the east, and the great flat expanse of the Dead Sea in between. All the rest is wilderness and sky.

A British explorer of the last century, Sir Francis Younghusband, caught the feeling of the desert when from the detachment of English urban life he wrote: "In Europe we look up into the sky between trees and houses; and among the clouds and through a murky atmosphere we see a few stars. Even when we have a clear sky we seldom get a chance of seeing the whole expanse of the heavens all the way round. . . . In the Gobi Desert . . . I often had the feeling of being more connected with the starry firmament than with this earth. . . . In a curious way the bodily and the material seemed to exist no longer, and I would be in spirit among the stars. My home was the whole great Cosmos."

Who has not known the same feeling on a mountaintop or on the open sea. "In the artificial world of his cities and towns [man] often forgets the true nature of his planet and the long vistas of its history," writes Rachel Carson. "The sense of these things comes to him most clearly in the course of a long ocean voyage, when he watches day after day the receding rim of the horizon . . . when at night he becomes aware of the earth's rotation as the stars pass overhead; or when alone in this world of water and sky he feels the loneliness of his earth in space."

If Wordsworth was right when he spoke of God as one "Whose dwelling is the light of setting suns"; if it is true that the presence of God is more felt than understood, in the broad rolling earth as seen from a mountaintop; in the infinity of the stars at night, or in the unconquerable reaches of the trackless sea; would not a sense of the presence of God become most clear out upon the desert. For the desert has all the qualities of the sunset and the sea, the mountaintop and the stars, and one more besides. That quality is stillness. There is no motion whatever in the desert, and no sound. There is only you, the hard desert floor upon which you stand, the stars over your head, and God. That is all. Freya Stark has written that the mystic retreats from the habitations of men "to seek a world where every object he sees is not wound in a cocoon of thought and images created by others. . . . The true call of the desert, of the mountains or the sea is their silence—free of the network of dead speech." Of all these only the desert is truly still.

It would be hard to overestimate the importance of the fact that the Children of Israel were a desert people. Only those who have been in the East and have known at first hand the blazing heat of an arid wilderness can imagine what it is like to live there. When Isaiah compares a righteous king to "the shadow of a great rock in a weary land," the desert traveler knows what he means. But a few hours in such a region will teach any traveler how precious the shadow of a rock—the only protection from the sun for miles around—may become. When we think of the hardihood the desert dwellers of three thousand years ago must have possessed in order to survive, we can imagine something of the mettle of the ancestors of the Jews. That alone, perhaps, is enough to account for their uncompromising attitude toward the moral law. Out in the desert wasteland, they lived too close to the edge of survival to permit any deviation from tribal precepts whatever.

The spiritual impact of the desert upon the early Hebrew tribes must have been at least as great as the moral. They never had any shelter but the tents they themselves made and put over their own heads. As a result, they lived their lives in the constant presence of the sun and the stars. The Milky Way and Orion, the North Star and Vega were more familiar to them than are the streets of our home town to us. We can only speculate upon the impact of this nightly experience upon them—the cool sweet night that always followed the misery of the day, when the sun rode over their heads in a burning cloudless sky. It was a poet, descended from these men of the desert, who long afterward gazed into the heavens and wondered, "When I consider the heavens, the work of thy fingers, the moon and the stars which thou hast ordained, what is man that thou art mindful of him?" The desert still lay close to this ancient singer— close because Palestine itself has always been a desertous region, but close too because the blood of men who knew no other kind of life still flowed in his veins.

It was out in the desert that the ancient Hebrews found the God they worshiped and because of this they found in him the qualities the desert instilled into them. In Yahweh they found immensity, the immensity of land that stretched away from them in every direction. They found in him regularity and dependability, the regularity they saw in the stars that wheeled over their heads each night, always in the same general pattern, and the dependability with which they, the night and the day always returned. As they watched, these ancient desert nomads knew that it had been so for generations; and that it would still be so long after their time. Then, as now, and as it had been long before, the same stars that always came to fill the night sky when the sun had made his circuit of the heavens, would come again. They would come exactly where they had always been and together they would sweep around the sky as they had always done and fade out when the sun came back to begin his journey again in the morning.

Out of the Jordanian desert, then, came the religion of Yahweh, a religion so strong, so noble, and so intimately woven into the fabric of Israel's mentality that it could evoke a lasting loyalty of her people. The worship of Yahweh generated within itself a fierce loyalty that brooked no rivals and yielded to no compromise. As the centuries passed, the ideal grew, but always the growth was generated from within. Always the new and greater ideal was the expression and development of what had been implicit in the old. That is why Israel's prophets usually thought they were calling the people back to an ancient standard even when their teaching offered something quite new.

The prophets always spoke in the name of Yahweh. This, as we have seen, was the reason for their special power and for the special immunity from harm they almost always enjoyed. We shall have to leave it to others to explain why these particular desert dwellers, the Hebrews, rather than any of the other desert dwellers of the ages, should have come into the possession of so great a religious tradition, why they, more than any others, came to look upon the Lord's prophets as sacred emissaries. Perhaps the explanation is the one most frequently given, that it came originally at the hands of a superb desert genius whose name was Moses. Whatever the answer to that question may be, it is the stern moral and spiritual quality of the desert religion of Israel that concerns us here. For it was in Israel's hour of trial that some of the latter-day devotees of Yahweh returned to the wilderness, lest in the encroachments of civilization upon them, they cease to live under the covenant formed between Yahweh and his people there a millennium before.

Surely none of the Essenes who went out as exiles from Jerusalem and built their Community Center in the wasteland of Qumran thought of themselves as returning to the desert in order to preserve the religion which had descended to them out of the desert in the first place. And yet are we stretching the truth when we say that this is what really happened? When we consider that the Essenes found in the desert the vital religion they sought, we can perhaps see that whether the Essenes realized it or not, when they returned to the wellsprings of their own religious life, they found there the essence of the religion of their fathers that had almost escaped them in the urban life of Jerusalem.

The Essene story, a nearly forgotten chapter in our history that only now is unfolding before our eyes, is by no means complete. Details are constantly being added and they will continue to be until all the Dead Sea Scrolls, including the fragment literature, has been analyzed, collated, and set in juxtaposition with such other relevant information as we already possess. As the data accumulates, and various attempts are made to interpret it, our understanding of the Essene story will be further increased.

But we should not minimize the fact that our picture is limited. Only a decade ago we had very little to go on. Until the discovery of the Dead Sea Scrolls, the Essenes were dismissed by our ablest scholars as a shadowy sectarian group of ascetics in Israel in the time of Jesus. Now we know that Christianity germinated, took root, and enjoyed its first growth in Essene soil. And we know that Christianity itself, in the beginning, was Essenic in character.

Now we know, too, that Christianity did not succeed Judaism, but that both religions share a common ancestry in the religion of ancient Israel. The distinction between the Old and the New Covenant—the Old and the New Testament—of which the early Christians made so much was not really original with them. It was a development of a concept the Essenes had worked out by which to justify their separation from the official religion of Israel. Contemporary Judaism is descended from the official Judaism of the Temple at Jerusalem and the Synagogues of the Diaspora of the first century B.C. and the first century A.D. Christianity is descended from sectarian Judaism of the same time, in particular from the sectarianism of the Essenes.

Thus, through the discovery of the Dead Sea Scrolls, we can now see that Judaism and Christianity need not be competitors vying with one another as to which is prior to the other. Neither is prior. Both are branches growing out of the same root. And both still bear within themselves the two tendencies the original division between them exemplifies. From the beginning both have exhibited priestly orthodox institutional elements, and both have exhibited aescetic, purist, sectarian, independent-minded tendencies. Both have heard the repeated demand for yet more holiness in the Temple, and both have seen men separate from the official Temple worship in search of a holiness the official religion could not or would not institute.

The demand made by the Essenes long ago in Israel had been voiced many times before by other men in other days. It has been heard many times since, and it will be heard again and again in the centuries to come. The vision of perfection enshrined in the religions of men constantly evokes from them a demand for yet more holiness and yet higher standards of conduct than the Temple requires. From time to time, stern courageous men filled with the love of God grow impatient with the compromises of the Temple. Then, driven out, departing voluntarily, or both, they seek elsewhere to live out in their own lives all that their religion has inspired them to believe and to do. Such men were the Essenes.

Notes

Page Line

16   21   Yigael Yadin, *The Scroll of the War of the Sons of Light against the Sons of Darkness* (in Hebrew), Jerusalem, Bialik Institute, 1956. See also Gaster, *op. cit.*, p. 277.

18   15   Burrows, *op. cit.*, 365.

20   2   *Ibid.*, p. 366.

20   34   *Ibid.*, p. 367.

22   17   *Ibid.*, p. 371.

24   1   *Ibid.*, p. 376.

24   13   Gaster, *Dead Sea Scriptures*, p. 104, n. 50, suggests that the mysterious and much-debated Book of Hagu mentioned in the Damascus Document is in reality the Essene Book of Psalms. However, he appears subsequently to have changed his mind on this point. In "The 'Sons of Light,'" *Commentary*, Sept., 1956, p. 233, he says the Book of Hagu is "evidently an official interpretation of Biblical law."

24   13   Charles T. Fritsch, *The Qumran Community*, New York, Macmillan, 1956, p. 80, believes the Manual of Discipline is the Book of Hagu.

24   31   Burrows, *op. cit.*, pp. 385-86.

26   24   Gen. 12:19.

26   27   *New York Times*, Nov. 9, 1956.

28   8   Wright Baker, "How the Dead Sea Scrolls were Opened," *Engineering*, April 13, 1956, pp. 194-96.

28   15   J. M. Allegro, *The Dead Sea Scrolls*, Harmondsworth, Middlesex, Penguin Books, 1956, pp. 181-84.

28   31   J. T. Milik, "The Copper Document from Cave IV Qumran," *Biblical Archaeologist*, Sept., 1956, pp. 62, 63.

29   10   *New York Times*, June 1, 1956, p. 1.

29   34   Milik, *op. cit.*, pp. 63, 64.

30   16   *Ibid.*, p. 64.

31   8   Frank M. Cross, Jr., "The Oldest Manuscripts from Qumran," *Journal of Biblical Literature*, Sept., 1955, p. 163.

31   35   Frank M. Cross, Jr., "A Report on the Biblical Fragments of Cave Four in Wadi Qumran," *Bulletin of the American Schools of Oriental Research*, Feb., 1956, p. 9.

3. THE ANCIENT HERITAGE OF THE ESSENES

33   1   Those who wish more detail on the events covered in this chapter should consult Emil Schurer, *History of the Jewish People in the Times of Jesus Christ*, Division I, New York, Scribner's, 1891. Abram L. Sachar, *History of the Jews*, New York, Knopf, 1940, and I. G. Mathews, *The Religious Pilgrimage of Israel*, New York, Harper, 1947, are good general accounts.

45   9   Quoted in Morton Scott Enslin, *Christian Beginnings*, New York, Harper, 1938, p. 13.

46   9   Fritsch, *op. cit.*, p. 83, argues that the author of the Damascus Document is trying to show by his elaborate chronology that Essene origins go back to the Hasidim.

Page Line

7. THE ESSENE COMMUNITY AT QUMRAN

80   4   Philo, *Quod Omnis Probus Liber,* s. 12.
80   5   Josephus, *Wars of the Jews,* Book II, VIII, 4.
80   11   Gaster, *Dead Sea Scriptures,* pp. 34 and 328.
80   25   Burrows, *op. cit.,* p. 374.
81   22   Rabin, *op. cit.,* p. 2.
82   29   Burrows, *op. cit.,* p. 372.
83   5   Donald W. Riddle, "The Martyrs, A Study in Social Control,"
          Univ. of Chicago, 1931.
84   2   Philo, *op. cit.,* s. 13.
85   3   Michael Evenari and Dov Koller, "Ancient Masters of the Desert,"
          Scientific American, April, 1956, p. 39.
86   16   H. H. Rowley, *The Zadokite Fragments,* Oxford, Blackwell, 1952,
          p. 51.
87   12   Josephus, *Wars,* Book II, VIII, 3.
87   13   Gaster, *Dead Sea Scriptures,* p. 231.
87   28   Josephus, *Wars,* Book II, VIII, 3.
87   33   A. DuPont-Sommer, *op. cit.,* p. 79.
88   6   *Ibid.,* p. 79.
88   25   *Ibid.,* p. 80.
90   2   Burrows, *op. cit.,* p. 378.
90   9   *Ibid.,* p. 371.
90   25   Rabin, *op. cit.,* pp. 58, 60, 70, 76.
90   26   Gaster, *Dead Sea Scriptures,* p. 307.
90   35   Josephus, *Wars,* Book II, VIII, 5.
91   22   Burrows, *op. cit.,* p. 373.

8. PIETY AND POLITICS

93   27   Burrows, *op. cit.,* p. 409.
94   30   *Ibid.,* p. 402.
95   27   Quoted in Schurer, *op. cit.,* p. 311.
98   22   Quoted in Enslin, *op. cit.,* pp. 38, 39.

9. THE COMMUNITY CENTER IS ABANDONED

106   6   Charles T. Fritsch, "Herod the Great and the Qumran Com-
           munity," *Journal of Biblical Literature,* Sept., 1955, p. 173.
108   18   Burrows, *op. cit.,* p. 372.
108   35   Hos. 4:16.
108   37   Rabin, *op. cit.,* p. 4.
110   6   Burrows, *op. cit.,* p. 368.
110   20   *Ibid.,* p. 365.
110   23   *Ibid.,* p. 367.
110   27   *Ibid.,* p. 369.
111   15   Rabin, *op. cit.,* p. 2.

10. WHERE WAS THE LAND OF DAMASCUS?

112   11   Rabin, *op. cit.,* p. 12.

Page Line

113   4   *Ibid.,* p. 24.
113   17 *Ibid.,* p. 2.
113   22 *Ibid.,* p. 2.
113   35 Ezek. 44:15.
114   2   Rabin, *op. cit.,* p. 12.
114   10 *Ibid.,* p. 22.
114   25 Burrows, *op. cit.,* p. 354.
115   20 Robert North, "The Damascus of Qumran Geography," *Palestine Exploration Quarterly,* April, 1955, p. 34.
116   3   Gaster, *Dead Sea Scriptures,* pp. 4, 101 n.23.
116   12 Zech 9:1.
116   12 J. M. Allegro, "Further Messianic References in Qumran Literature," *Journal of Biblical Literature,* Sept., 1956, p. 175.
118   12 Ezek. 16:60, 61.
118   25 Gaster, *Dead Sea Scriptures,* pp. 4, 103 n.40.

11. THE RETURN

126   22 Enslin, *op. cit.,* p. 62.
128   22 J. M. Allegro, "A Newly Discovered Fragment of a Commentary on Ps. 37 from Qumran," *Palestine Exploration Quarterly,* May-Oct., 1954, p. 69.
131   33 Burrows, *op. cit.,* p. 377.

12. JOHN THE BAPTIST

134   8   Luke 7:28.
134   11 Luke 3:7, 8, 9, 10, 11.
136   18 James Hastings, *Dictionary of the Bible,* New York, Scribner's, 1900, Vol. I, p. 770.
137   3   Matt. 3:3.
137   3   Mark 1:3.
137   3   Luke 3:4.
137   3   John 1:23.
137   8   Burrows, *op. cit.,* p. 382.
137   17 "Day of Yahweh": See Amos 5:18, 20; Isa. 2:12, 13:6, 9, 34:8; Jer. 46:10; Zeph. 1:7, 2:2, 3; Zech. 14:1; Joel 1:15, 2:1; Mal. 4:5.
137   22 The "Branch": See Deut. 18:8; Isa. 11:1; Jer. 23:5; Zech. 3:8.
138   13 Carl Kraeling, *John the Baptist,* New York, Scribner's, 1951, p. 117.
138   23 Dan. 7:9, 13.
139   31 Burrows, *op. cit.,* p. 383.
139   32 See Gaster, "The 'Sons of Light,'" *op. cit.,* p. 229.
139   34 Rabin, *op. cit.,* p. 36.
140   4   J. M. Allegro, "A Newly Discovered Fragment," *op. cit.,* p. 71.
140   6   Rabin, *op. cit.,* p. 32.
140   7   *Ibid.,* p. 42.
140   11 Burrows, *op. cit.,* p. 377.
140   16 *Ibid.,* p. 373.
141   1   Burrows, *op. cit.,* p. 373.

Page Line

14. DIFFERENCES BETWEEN JESUS AND THE ESSENES

154   6   Matt. 5:33-37.
154   13   Burrows, *op. cit.*, p. 377.
154   17   Rabin, *op. cit.*, pp. 70, 72, 74, 76.
155   3   Cf. Gaster, *The Dead Sea Scriptures*, p. 96 n.43.
155   16   Luke 6:40.
155   20   Luke 9:46-48.
155   24   Luke 14:7 ff.
155   28   Mark 10:35-45.
155   37   Burrows, *op. cit.*, p. 378.
156   13   Matt. 8:20.
156   23   Matt. 11:19.
156   30   Matt. 5:44.
156   31   Burrows, *op. cit.*, 371.
156   37   Matt. 5:43-48.
157   18   Matt. 5:20.
157   20   Matt. 5:6.
157   21   Matt. 6:33.
157   29   Mark 3:4.
157   32   Mark 2:27.
157   37   Burrows, *op. cit.*, pp. 359 ff. Cf. Rabin, *op. cit.*, pp. 52 ff.
158   30   Burrows, *op. cit.*, p. 373.
158   31   *Ibid.*, p. 377.
158   32   Rabin, *op. cit.*, p. 50.
159   1   Luke 7:36-50.
159   6   Matt. 9:10-13.
159   11   Mark 7:1-23.
160   1   Matt. 23:16-22.
160   19   Matt. 23:1-3. The quotation is from the King James Version,
             which is clearer here than the Revised Standard Version.
161   14   Matt. 5:17.
162   10   Matt. 23:23-24.
162   16   Matt. 5:21-28.

15. THE MEANING OF THE SIMILARITIES AND DIFFERENCES BETWEEN
JESUS AND THE ESSENES

163   8   Schweitzer, *op. cit.*
164   11   Ernest Renan, *Life of Jesus*, Boston, Little, Brown, 1924, transla-
             tion revised from the 23rd French edition.
164   17   James Moffatt in E.R.E., Vol. V, p. 400.
164   32   Carl Kraeling, *John the Baptist*, pp. 108-9.
166   10   Mark 1:2-11; 6:14-29.
166   16   Mark 6:14-29.
166   21   Mark 8:27-30.
166   37   Oscar Cullmann, "The Significance of the Qumran Texts for
             Research into the Beginnings of Christianity," *Journal of Bibli-
             cal Literature*, Dec., 1955, p. 213.

Page Line

167   6   John 1:19-42.
168   1   John 10:1-8 *passim.*
168   15 I John 1:18-22; 4:1-6.
170   1   Wilfred Sheed, "The Dead Sea Scrolls and the Living Church,"
          Trumpet, Apr.-May, 1956, p. 1.
171   5   Editorial in *The Living Church,* Feb. 19, 1956, p. 11.

16. THE SIMILARITIES BETWEEN THE ESSENES AND THE EARLY CHRISTIAN CHURCH

173   1   Gaster, "The 'Sons of Light,'" *op. cit.,* p. 234. See also *Dead Sea
          Scriptures,* pp. 12 ff. and 35.
174   8   Matt. 18:15-18.
175   22 Burrows, *op. cit.,* p. 384.
175   30 Frank Cross, "The Scrolls and the New Testament," *Christian
          Century,* Aug. 24, 1955, p. 968.
175   36 Luke 2:14.
176   2   Cross, "The Scrolls and the New Testament," p. 968.
176   12 *Ibid.,* p. 971.
176   33 Krister Stendahl, *The School of St. Matthew,* Uppsala, 1954.
178   4   Lucetta Mowry, "The Dead Sea Scrolls and the Background for
          the Gospel of John," *Biblical Archaeologist,* Dec., 1954, p. 78.
178   19 Burrows, *op. cit.,* pp. 238-42.
178   30 Cf. Fritsch, *Qumran Community,* p. 85, and Allegro, *The Dead
          Sea Scrolls,* pp. 112-14, 116-18.
178   31 Fritsch, *Qumran Community,* pp. 116 ff., lists several of these
          parallels.
179   22 Gaster, *Dead Sea Scriptures,* p. 15.
179   22 *Ibid.,* p. 17.
179   36 Sherman E. Johnson, "The Dead Sea Manual of Discipline and the
          Jerusalem Church of Acts," *Zeitschrift fur die Alttestementliche
          Wissenschoft,* Vol. 66, 1954, p. 106.
180   33 Luke 22:29, 30.
181   16 Acts 7:57, 58.
181   19 Acts 7:51-53.
181   28 Burrows, *op. cit.,* p. 376.
182   23 See Cross, "The Scrolls and the New Testament," *op. cit.,* p. 968,
          and A. Dupont-Sommer, *op. cit.,* pp. 77 ff.
182   25 Quoted by Cross, *Ibid.,* p. 969.
183   7   *Idem.*
183   14 Gaster, *Dead Sea Scriptures,* pp. 19 ff. and 279, thinks the "Mes-
          sianic Banquet" theory untenable. Whatever the resolution of this
          particular point may be, all agree with Gaster in emphasizing the
          fact that the Essene meal was primarily an agape feast and not
          communion in the later Christian sense of the word.

17. THE MEANING OF THE SIMILARITIES BETWEEN THE ESSENES
AND THE EARLY CHRISTIAN CHURCH

184   4   See Gaster, *Dead Sea Scriptures,* pp. 18-20.

Page Line

186   7   Acts 4:13.

188 32 Walter J. Harrelson, "The Human Side of the Dead Sea Scrolls," *Advance,* June 27, 1956, p. 6.

191   2 Acts 5:36, 37.

191 25 Josephus, *Wars,* Book II, VIII, 10.

192   3 Cullmann, *op. cit.,* pp. 213 ff.

193   7 Acts 5:38-39.

18. PROPHETS IN THE GREAT TRADITION

198 23 Francis Younghusband, *The Heart of Nature,* London, John Murray, 1921, pp. 115-17.

198 34 Rachel Carson, *The Sea Around Us,* Oxford, 1951, p. 15.

199   5 William Wordsworth, "Tintern Abbey."

199 17 Freya Stark, *Perseus in the Wind,* London, John Murray, 1948, pp. 6. 7.

199 26 Isa. 32:2.

200 12 Ps. 8:3.

INDEX